DVCAM

A Practical Guide
to the Professional System

Also by the same author:

Shooting Digital Video (Focal Press)
Arriflex 16SR Book (Focal Press)
Arriflex 35 Book (Focal Press)
Arriflex 16 SR3: The Book
Arriflex 435 Book
ARRI 16SR Book
ARRI 35 Book

DVCAM

A Practical Guide
to the Professional System

Jon Fauer, ASC

Focal Press
Taylor & Francis Group

NEW YORK AND LONDON

First published 2001

This edition published 2013
by Focal Press
70 Blanchard Road, Suite 402, Burlington, MA 01803

Simultaneously published in the UK
by Focal Press
2 Park Square, Milton Park, Abingdon, Oxon OX14 4RN

Focal Press is an imprint of the Taylor & Francis Group, an informa business

ISBN 13: 978-0-240-80480-4 (pbk)

Transferred to Digital Printing in 2014

Table of Contents

Foreword

The successful establishment of a professional digital recording format is highly dependent upon many factors. These include the timing of the format's introduction, the technologies involved, technical performance achieved, emergence of early leaders and sustained growth of the related product family.

DVCAM has emerged as the fastest growing professional recording format in Sony's history. If success is measured by market penetration, then analog Betacam earlier held that distinction, having reached 440,000 total units shipped worldwide over its seventeen-year life to date. DVCAM has already reached 230,000 units (as of August, 2001) in the five short years since its first introduction at the 1996 NAB. The format had reached sales of 100,000 units by 1999, which then sharply accelerated—more than doubling within the next 15 months.

A number of factors have contributed to this rapid marketplace acceptance of DVCAM. The communications industry at large is accelerating its transition to digital acquisition and postproduction, and the technical performance of this digital format definitively surpasses all former analog formats (U-matic, S-VHS, Hi8, etc).

In addition, low cost desktop nonlinear editing systems are proliferating, and the incorporation of the powerful i.LINK/IEEE 1394 interface into the DVCAM camcorders and VTRs has built the crucial bridge to these systems. This, in turn, is stimulating increased diversity in production.

Digital filmmaking has recently acquired an almost cult status and innovative new communication businesses are springing up all over. Realizing all of this, Sony has progressively broadened the DVCAM family to an unprecedented range of product offerings. As this book will amply demonstrate, DVCAM today meets virtually all needs and all budgets—in both DVCAM acquisition and in the associated editing recorders and players.

The technical underpinnings of DVCAM are a set of specific attributes that distinctly set this format apart from its consumer DV parent-attributes which collectively define all that we mean by "professional" when describing a recording format. These attributes were defined by the distinguished engineering teams that had, over the past several decades, developed and refined the first professional workhorse recording formats—notably the U-matic and Betacam formats—which had sharply focused on the diverse needs of the business, corporate, and industrial sectors of the communications world.

This book will go into considerable detail in outlining how all that collectively comes together to define the new digital professional format that we call DVCAM.

Yet, the beauty of DVCAM is that a very close compatibility was still carefully maintained with the parent consumer DV format. This was a special design priority that recognized the blurring of formerly sharp distinctions between high-end consumer and the lower-budget professional formats. The broad expansion in picture and sound acquisition needs of the past decade spawned a philosophy that low-cost consumer digital camcorders might have important roles to play within professional applications (all the way up to broadcast news).

The rise of the professional consumer (or "Prosumer" as they are sometimes affectionately dubbed) would also see the lower end professional products being harnessed to spawn innovative new businesses. With that marketplace dynamic in mind, Sony made specific design alterations within the DVCAM recording format that increased the integrity of digital capture over a wide range of environmental conditions, as well as adding time code and other features and facilities important to the professional. But, some of the DVCAM camcorders can also be switched to record in DV, should that need arise. DVCAM decks can play back tapes that were originated in DV consumer camcorders. Thus, when required, end users can mix and match the DV and DVCAM equipment to extend the breadth of their applications.

While the birth of DVCAM was propelled by needs in the broader professional video markets, Sony was also paying close attention to the broadcasters as they plotted their various transition paths into our unique new multiformat digital DTV era. While the ½-inch recording platform forms the mainstay of their digital ENG and Production broadcast needs, there was a visible demand for lower cost and more mobile acquisition systems to flank their mainstream DTV systems. Sony produced the Master Series of DVCAM VTRs to meet these needs and to encompass all variants of DV recordings.

DVCAM and other digital recording formats exhibit the startling clarity of picture and sound capture that they do as a consequence of advanced technological refinements in the science of magnetic tape recording. The central role of contemporary digital recording media is deemed so important to the art of digital picture-making that special attention is paid in this book to explaining these recent advances.

A continuing dilemma for the manufacturer who develops sophisticated products and systems like DVCAM is making them user-friendly. We do engage in ongoing dialog with those who use our products, and every new generation reflects innovations and features suggested by the production community. A challenge remains, however, in effectively explaining the many important facets of our products, and describing all that differentiates one camcorder or VTR from the others within that product family. Our brochures and manuals tend to be dry and factual—and, to some, even intimidating. It seemed to make good sense to seek a writer who is immersed in the use of our products, and request that writer to speak to demystify them, in language and style that is familiar to the creative production world, and hopefully minimizes technical jargon.

Jon Fauer, ASC is uniquely qualified to create a book dedicated to informing on all facets of this very flexible digital recording family. Over many years he has written a broad and highly popular series of books on film cameras and filmmaking. He is recognized for his particular skill in demystifying the subtle complexities of both and in imparting detailed information on operating and maintaining high-end film cameras. He has developed a special approach to imparting a lot of complex information in an engaging and user-friendly manner—a manner guaranteed to ensure the close attention of the reader. Sony was impressed by Jon's recent publication *Shooting Digital Video*, his first foray into a book on digital technology, and one that clearly struck the right note in explaining contemporary digital shooting to a wide audience. We asked Jon to consider a more in-depth treatise of our own DVCAM technology and product family, and specifically requested that he utilize his own unique methods, his humor and his anecdotes to outline the new empowerments that digital acquisition and editing offers to an increasingly large and diverse production community. We believe the reader will see that this fine work is among his best. Jon Fauer has done us all a service in building an important communication bridge between those who create powerful but complex products and those who turn these into an art form.

It is Sony's hope that the publication of a book like this will begin an increasing dialog between us and all who make programs of so many forms on the DVCAM format. Our developments continue, and we are eager to shape those developments according to the real needs of our many end-users.

Laurence J. Thorpe
Senior Vice President, Acquisition Systems
Sony Broadcast and Professional Company

Robert L. Ott
Vice President, VTR/Storage Products
Sony Broadcast and Professional Company

4   *DVCAM*

Introduction

Democratization

DVCAM, the professional version of DV, is at the forefront of an incredible democratization that is empowering more people than ever dreamed possible to see, record, edit, and ultimately share their vision with an audience of breathtaking size. Its popularity among vastly different users—students, network news organizations, educational, corporate and legal producers, event videographers, independent filmmakers, government organizations, human rights groups and ordinary citizens is a testament to the democracy of a new and rapidly growing format.

Who could have predicted, when film was viewed as a flickering image the size of a postage stamp on a Kinetoscope, that over a century later anyone with an internet connection, anywhere in the world, would have the opportunity to view digital moving images delivered on demand?

Most historians agree that George Eastman and Thomas Edison met in 1889 to discuss the specifications for Edison's Kinetoscope. George Eastman is said to have asked "how wide?" Thomas Edison held up his thumb and forefinger. The motion picture format devised from that meeting was 35 millimeters (1 3/8 inches) wide, with four rectangular perforations on each side of each frame—almost the same dimensions and specifications still in use today.

Film in the twentieth century brought universal ideas to the largest audience in history, became a common bond, one of the most powerful art forms, and influenced the globalization of nations, corporations and ideas. It was a century in which ideas could be presented to ever larger numbers of people in ever shorter spans of time. Never before had so many people sat together to watch the same moving images, to share the same common bonds, dreams, universal themes and emotions, shared across the boundaries of nations, language, and social structure.

Over one hundred years ago, the first cinematographers set off to film the world around them. Early locations were the Panama Canal, Egypt, New York, Paris, Berlin, London.

One hundred and four years after Eastman and Edison met to discuss a new motion picture format, ten companies met to discuss a new digital motion imaging format. Two years later, fifty-five companies agreed on the new consumer DV format. A year after that, Sony introduced its professional version, DVCAM. The new century holds prospects of novel applications for motion imaging. The new digital images can be viewed on television, computer, personal digital devices or large movie screens.

Dimaging

But first, we need some new terminology that transcends an epithet ascribed to recording digital video: "capturing," as in "we captured some awesome shots today." With apologies to Nabokov, no butterly nets were used, nor, we trust, were wild creatures harmed in the gathering of wild photons. Perhaps we're trying to render a process once called "shooting" less intimidating; there certainly are more of us doing it. Even the designation "video" is an understatement. Consider the path of a project that originates on DVCAM, digitally recorded on magnetic tape, sent by i.LINK cable to a computer's hard drive where it is edited and output concurrently to DVD, streamed on the internet, and recorded to film. Is it video, or film, or digital motion imaging—dimaging?

In the ineluctable democratization of visual expression, even traditional professional job descriptions are changing. If cinematographers are shooting on DVCAM—the professional digital video format, should we be called videographers? And when the digital master is then "printed" by laser onto 35mm motion picture film to be projected in movie theatres, do we become cinematographers again? Should the cinematographer who shoots film for a television commercial that is scanned onto a digital master be called something entirely different from the documentary cameraman shooting DVCAM for the show which the television commercial is sponsoring?

At the convergence of silver halides and binary bits, along with the new methodologies, a new vocabulary is emerging. Most urgent is finding a word to replace "capturing." For the moment, I can't think of anything better than "dimaging."

It has been lamented by some that the democratization of motion imaging has led to an abundance of film schools, students, workshops, instructional materials, books (uh-oh), and a large pool of less experienced, but eminently qualified and enthusiastic, proponents. Although DVCAM camcorders can "capture" an image quickly in automatic or EZ Mode, these are highly sophisticated and technically advanced instruments with a huge pallette of manual controls and visual adjustments. DVCAM has become a universal medium. It is being used by professionals and prosumers, film students and independent feature crews. It is used by schools to record first plays, and by news crews to broadcast the first news of the day around the world.

The fact that more people are using it than ever before should not be cause for alarm. Personal computers democratized the task of writing with word processing. The fact that any pre-school toddler can hit a keyboard and come up with letters on the screen has not caused the demise of global literature. I feel equally optimistic about dimaging because it is also a tool to transform ideas into images, using technology customized to the task.

About this Book

This book is an overview of the DVCAM format and its equipment. It is written from the perspective of a user. I tried to write as if I were explaining how to use the equipment to a friend or colleague standing next to me—the way I would try to demonstrate it in a workshop or class.

This book doesn't pretend to be totally comprehensive, or answer every question. But, I do hope this book answers the main questions that arise in the course of actual production, from the perspective of a cameraman who uses the equipment.

Our business can be pretty stressful. Cinematographers often reassure each other that "it isn't brain surgery." Then there's the joke about the brain surgeon who's about to operate on a cinematographer. The surgeon is stressed out: hands trembling, beads of sweat on brow. The cameraman looks up and says: "Relax, Doc. We're not shooting a TV commercial."

The foremost textbook on brain surgery, *Neuroanatomy*, by Richard L. Sidman, begins by pretending the reader is in Kindergarten. There's a picture of the brain, and the text asks you to fill in the blank: "This is a picture of the _____." You are tricked into thinking that brain surgery really isn't that difficult. With each chapter, the authors graduate you to a higher grade. Eventually you get into medical school, and by then you thoroughly understand the workings of the brain.

I have tried to take a similar approach with my previous books on cameras. To be as comprehensive as possible, at the risk of offending advanced users, but to make it fun to read, we usually begin by assuming the reader is a total novice and doesn't know which end of a soldering iron to hold. If it works for brain surgeons, certainly it can be useful for camera people.

Instruction manuals rarely travel with the equipment for which they were intended. The original manuals for Sony DVCAM camcorders are comprehensive and quite good. You can order them from a toll-free telephone number, and they will ship to you by Fedex. I encourage you to read the Sony manual for the camera you're using. However, the chances are good that the manual will still be back at the office when you're ready to roll, and you can't remember whether you should be in progressive scan or interlace mode.

In the summer of 2000, Focal Press asked me to write *Shooting Digital Video* for consumers and prosumers. We had already worked together on books about the motion picture cameras I owned, so I thought the new book should deal with the DV and DVCAM camcorders I was just beginning to use. This equipment happened to be made by Sony.

I've been a fan of Sony ever since I was a boy. They had a New York showroom on 47th Street and Fifth Avenue. It was always packed. We can only guess whether the throngs were drawn by Sony's new "tummy-TV," as the ads called their beautifully-designed, five-inch wide, micro-TV, or the stunning fashion models Mr. Morita had hired to demonstrate the products. However, my classmates and I made almost daily pilgrimages from 77th Street to 47th Street to gawk. And my father, a consummate gadgeteer, must have been spending an equal amount of time there, since he brought home what must have been one of every product Sony was making.

So, we had a history together, Sony and I. This is the holy grail of marketing and advertising, "branding" to the point where consumers trust a company so much they will buy the company's products because of the name. In Sony's case, the name stood for brilliant design, flawless construction and reliable service.

My books on cinematography have been nuts-and-bolts, how-to guides on using complex cameras that cost as much as a house, but usually travel with less documentation than the Space Shuttle. I assumed that *Shooting Digital Video* would follow that model, a how-to guide on consumer and a few prosumer Sony digital camcorders. However, the publishers and editors felt that we should not be exclusive, and we were obliged to include all competing companies and most of their products.

Shooting Digital Video was an overview of DV, DVCAM and DVCPRO. Its theme was how to choose a camcorder, and how to take begin using it. It was intended for beginners, consumers, prosumers and especially film people taking the first steps into the world of digital motion imaging. A few chapters on theory and one of the cameras are repurposed here.

This book is the one I originally intended to write. It is about DVCAM, and it's intended for prosumers and professionals who want to learn more about the format, want to figure out what equipment to use, how the different models compare, and how to use them.

Since it was introduced in 1996, over 230,000 DVCAM camcorders and VTRs have been sold worldwide. By comparison, about 440,000 Betacam machines have been sold in the last 17 years. The success of the DVCAM format is, not to be melodramatic, amazing. It began as a format intended to bring DV picture quality and ease of use to corporate users, and from there was applied to the harsh broadcast and professional environment.

Learning by Example

In some of my previous books, we tried to keep the reader awake with tales of the World's Worst Assistant, a character originally created by camera assistant Scott Rathner when he and I were marooned on a tropical island with cameras, agency, clients, rising tides, hungry insects, blowing sand and scorching sun.

Reading Gabriel García Márquez' *Love in the Time of Cholera* one sleepless trans-Pacific flight night, it occurred to me that a more magical-realist literary style might help. The World's Worst Cameraman was born— a character of such monumental ineptitude, concocted from horror stories both experienced and reported, he might actually make learning all kinds of dry camera and equipment facts fun. Joseph Losey, one of my mentors in college and director of *The Servant, The Go Between* and many other films, said "to educate, you have to entertain." I hope I have made a sufficient attempt.

The World's Worst Cameraman got into the business by accident. He then bluffed his way into film school, as a "legacy" whose relatives Rusty Gates, Dusty Gates, and Buzz Focus supposedly had distinguished themselves years before. Upon graduation, his frequent changes in residence were dictated by the repetition of warnings "you'll never work in this town again" from the producers of jobs he bungled.

It should be noted that The World's Worst Cameraman is in no way related to, nor role-modeled after, anyone in particular. He is, instead, a walking compendium of the worst nightmares in the business and he certainly makes me feel less chagrined when I can't remember which switch does what.

Like some of my other books, this one began with an urgent phone call asking where to find information on a camera I hadn't written about yet. In the story that follows, I hadn't yet begun the book on DVCAM you are reading now. As always, the names have been changed to protect the guilty—and the World's Worst Cameraman is off on a new adventure with some new DVCAM equipment.

Once upon a time, the World's Worst Cameraman figures he might try expanding his horizons by working as an actor on an independent feature. The director does not have much trouble casting him for the part of a dissembling scoundrel. It's the first day of the shoot, 5 am. Cast and crew are huddled around the craft-service table of foul coffee, stale bagels and spoiled milk. The production department is in panic mode. The Director of Photography has just called. He says he's shown up at the location specified on his call sheet, but can't find the rest of the crew.

"Where are you?" the production manager asks.

"A hundred miles north of the Arctic Circle," he says.

After much confusion, the facts emerge. Someone has given the DP the wrong call sheet and travel instructions. He's in the middle of nowhere. He won't be back for some time. But the production must go on.

The World's Worst Cameraman hides a satisfied smile. His big chance has arrived. Feigning great concern while balancing bagel, coffee and cell phone simultaneously in one hand, he casually mentions that prior to his career in acting he was actually a shooter. A PA tells an AD who calls the UPM who tells the Producer. The producer steers the World's Worst Cameraman away from the snack table to a nearby van with several cardboard boxes of unopened DVCAM equipment.

"What's your name?" the producer asks.

"You can call me WC," the World's Worst Cameraman says.

"Well, WC, this is our DSR-500WS," the producer says. "The thing is, when this job is done, we need to sell it to buy the editing equipment. So, we're counting on you to keep it in mint condition.

WC, the World's Worst Cameraman, gulps. Unfortunately, his previous work has been with a DSR-PD100A, and his experience is hardly vast. He used a DSR-250 once, at his own wedding. He's never even laid eyes on a DSR-500WS.

"Why didn't you rent the camera?" WC asks, stalling for time.

"Rental houses want a deposit. You think we have that kind of money? We buy the camera, put it on the credit card, and we'll sell it before the monthly statement comes in." The producer fans out the stack of credit cards that are financing the feature, and continues "The nice folks at T&A Photo recommended this. When they heard we were doing a feature, they said I shouldn't even think about trying to return the camera within the 14 day money-back period, after shooting the picture. The camera has a time-used counter, and if it has more than 350 hours, they're going to charge me a 15% restocking fee. But there are only 336 hours in 14 days. If only I could work the crew around the clock, night and day. Maybe it could be done with a day shift and a night shift. Maybe..."

"I don't think we can shoot this in 14 days," WC says.

"No, maybe not. But remember, WC. No scratches. No dings," the producer says.

WC has ten minutes to figure out how to use the DSR-500WS, and how to look like he knows what he's doing. Hopefully this book can help him.

Inevitably, even our worst fears pale in comparison with actual events. My first book was inspired by a Volkswagen repair manual, which advertising guru Alastair Riach offered as a paradigm of fun instruction. We included several expanded views of a camera to show how things worked. Unfortunately, several readers attempted to dissect their cameras exactly as depicted, with regrettable results.

While the majority of readers are experienced professionals, we nonetheless have to recognize the needs of film students and beginners as well. So, we pretend that the reader has just picked up a DVCAM camcorder for the first time, having just had one thrust into his or her hands, or having just made an impetuous mid-life career change from a previously sheltered life in investment banking or politics.

Some of the information and methods described herein are not endorsed by Sony. Just as some television spots often have the disclaimer "professional stuntman, do not attempt"—we occasionally put cameras and equipment into situations that make the designers and repair people cringe, especially when something goes wrong, and the mangled, tangled camera body is sheepishly brought into the repair department.

This book is for anyone planning to use Sony DVCAM equipment: student, consumer, prosumer, or professional. Welcome to DVCAM.

Disclaimer

Since these are litigious times, the inevitable disclaimer must be made. Some of the recommendations, specifications, modifications, accessories and procedures described in this book may not be accurate, nor have they necessarily been tested or approved by the manufacturers. As such, following my advice may void the warranty on the camera, the service contract, or the rental house agreement. It worked for me, but there is always the potential for misprints and errors.

Ask ten camera people to describe their style of shooting, and ten totally different opinions will emerge. Ask a dozen engineers to describe a perfect scene, and a dozen different scenarios will be imagined. Take the different styles, configure different looks to accommodate those styles, pack ten camcorders in ten different cases for ten different jobs, multiply by several thousand, and the chance that not everyone will agree with some of the suggestions in this book is almost comforting.

Although the text was meticulously checked by many people at Sony, typos and errors may still lurk within these pages, especially if I accidentally missed some of the corrections. Shooting a test is recommended whenever there is ever any doubt. Although we have made every attempt to check the facts and techniques described in this text, there still is the possibility of error, for which we apologize, but are not responsible or liable. Please let us know for future editions or update notices.

Conventions

CAMERA PARTS are identified in bold, uppercase Helvetica.

LCD and VIEWFINDER TEXT is indicated in uppercase New Century Schoolbook.

Despite Jimmy Carter's promise to have the United States on the metric standard by the end of his presidency, we still think in terms of feet, inches and pounds. I have tried to remember to include both English and metric. My apologies where forgotten.

Trademarks

Sony, Betacam SP, Betacam SX, Clear Scan, ClipLink, Digital 8, DVCAM logo, DVgate, DynaLatitude, EditStation, Hi8, Handycam, i.LINK, Memory Stick, QSDI, Remote Commander, SteadyShot, SetupLog, SetupNavi, TruEye, U-matic, VAIO, Video Walkman, Video 8 and XPRI are trademarks of Sony.

Windows is a registered trademark licensed to Microsoft Corporation, registered in the U.S.A. and other countries.

Macintosh, FireWire, Final Cut Pro, iMovie, Mac, iMac, iBook, Powerbook and Mac OS are trademarks of Apple Computer, Inc.

All other product names mentioned in this book may be the trademarks or registered trademarks of their respective companies.

Furthermore, "™" and "®" are not mentioned in each case in this book.

DSR-PD150

What is DVCAM?

DVCAM - How it began

This book is about DVCAM, the professional video standard developed by Sony, based on the popular DV format. It's useful to know how DVCAM began, and how it compares with DV, DVCPRO, and other video formats.

DV officially began on July 1, 1993, when ten companies (Sony, Mutsushita, Philips, Thomson, Toshiba, Hitachi, JVC, Sanyo, Sharp and Mitsubishi) joined together to form the HD Digital VCR Consortium. By 1995, over 55 companies had signed on, and the new consumer DV format came out later that year. Its main purpose was to replace Hi8. Sony introduced DVCAM a year later, in 1996.

I think Sony's first DV camcorder was the consumer DSR-PC7. I remember shooting a commercial for a major consumer electronics retailer and being so impressed that I traded some of my time for one of the camcorders. It was incredible.

DV was exciting because it truly was the first moving picture format that was relatively inexpensive and really easy to use. A Mini DV cassette, less than 1/12 the size of a standard VHS tape, could record up to an hour of material.

Easy in—easy out. VHS and Hi8 Video Cassettes were almost as easy to record, albeit larger. But not so easy to get out. You usually edited the tape on a linear tape-to-tape system. The quality became degraded each time it was copied, and by the time you went down a few generations, it looked like it was shot through Scotch Tape. The other alternative was a nonlinear editing system requiring you to digitize the picture (convert it from analog to digital), and then compress it with expensive hardware.

DV and DVCAM are compressed 5:1. The signal is digital. You just plug a FireWire/IEEE 1394/i.Link cable into your computer, click a couple of buttons, and the entire digital stream is copied directly from the camcorder to the hard drive in real or 4x time. There is no loss of quality. Distribution can be as simple as uploading a file to the web, for all to see.

One of digital video's universal appeals is its use of the computer and inexpensive editing software. Not since the personal computer replaced typewriters has there been such a democratization of a creative process. DV editing software is becoming as widely used as word processing software, with similar paradigms of cut and paste.

Five years ago, a high-end Avid or Media 100 nonlinear editing system cost anywhere from $20 to $100 thousand dollars. Recent editing software, while admittedly not as powerful, comes free with various new computers, or can be downloaded from the web. Final Cut Pro costs $990, and Avid Xpress DV is $1,699.

What's the Difference Between DVCAM and DV?

Let's answer the big questions right away: "What's the difference between DVCAM and DV? Why spend a little more money on a DVCAM camcorder or VTR, when DV is supposed to do the same thing—and what does DVCAM give me that DV will not?"

The short answer is one word: "TAPE."

That sounds almost as glib as the famous line in "The Graduate," where a family friend (William Daniels, now president of the Screen Actors Guild) tells Ben (Dustin Hoffman) that he has just one word for him: "PLASTICS."

The slightly longer answer, "tape and the hardware used to record and play it" is the main difference between professional DVCAM and consumer DV. DVCAM tape is more durable, more resistant to stretching, scratching, and dropouts, more precisely manufactured—and specifically intended for professional applications.

DVCAM and DV use the same size cassettes. There are two sizes: Standard (about the size of a pack of playing cards) and Mini (about the size of a pack of Tic-Tac breath mints). DVCAM and DV both use magnetic tape of the same width (6.35mm — 1/4"). But that's just the beginning.

There's an analogy in the 1/2" format. Digital Betacam, and Betacam SP use tape that's the same width as the original Betamax consumer format. However, the professional version travels faster. The track pitch (width of recorded information) is wider. The tape is manufactured to tighter tolerances and features professional enhancements. Overall specifications are matched to professional environments.

Essentially, the DVCAM format is a more rugged version of DV, capable of withstanding the rigors of location work under widely varying physical and environmental conditions. It provides even more reliable video and audio, frame-accurate editing, locked audio, along with the fail-safe capability of repeated handling during post production. Does this mean that we professionals tend to abuse our equipment more than hobbyists? I have been told by equipment managers at several film schools that professional wear and tear on cameras is nothing compared to the suffering inflicting by students.

My favorite tale of woe is the student who tried to pry an attached lens from a camcorder using a crowbar. "But I thought the lens was removable," he said later. Added durability is one of the reasons we're seeing more and more DVCAM equipment on campuses, although not even DVCAM is resistant to the abuse of crowbars.

I think the main difference between DVCAM and DV can be summarized by looking at the track pitch (the distance between the center of two adjacent tracks).

DVCAM, has a track pitch of 15 microns. The electron microscope photo at right compares the tracks on DVCAM and DV tapes.

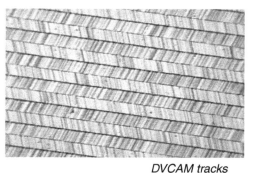

DVCAM tracks

DV has a narrower track pitch of 10 microns. By the way, a human hair is usually 60 microns thick—so these tracks of digital magnetic information are tiny.

We'll go over DVCAM's greater track pitch, width and technical matters in greater detail in the Theory chapter at the end of the book.

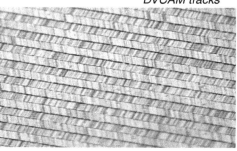

DV tracks

Imagine you're the magnetic head on a DVCAM camcorder. You're about the size of six quarters stacked on top of each other, and you're spinning around at 9,000 RPM.

Remember, this is a digital format—so all you have to worry about is finding or recording binary information on the tape. The tape is magnetized to represent ones and zeroes. Nevertheless, you have to deal with about 3.6 million of these ones and zeroes each second.

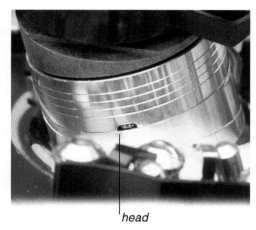

head

Now, imagine what happens to you, the video head, if the camera in which you are working happens to be filming a behind-the-scenes documentary of *A Perfect Storm*. Being a machine, you don't feel as bad as the camera operator: wet, cold and miserable. But salt water spray, wind, rain and violent camera movement are all attempting to make the image as ephemeral as possible. If just one grain of salt comes between you and the tape, you have a problem. That single grain of salt could be bigger than the area of tape onto which you want to record. So, which would you rather have: a 15 micron-wide DVCAM track or a mere 10 micron-wide DV track?

Having completed *A Perfect Storm*, we're now doing an independent feature, based on *Lawrence of Arabia*. We have secured the rights, but it's 130° in the shade, and there is no shade. When environmental conditions are extreme, when things change, if the tape head has somehow managed to become slightly misaligned—wouldn't we rather have a bigger area in which to work?

DVCAM's wider area of recorded information provides a greater safety margin against dropout, tape expansion or contraction, misaligned heads, humidity, extreme temperatures and all kinds of other environmental factors conspiring against the physics of image acquisition. As we shall see, the beauty of DVCAM is that while specifically designed to meet these demanding professional extremes, the format is also very compatible with the consumer DV "parent."

Sony originally developed DVCAM for the business and corporate markets, which previously had used 3/4", Hi8 and Betacam SP. Smaller broadcast and cable stations soon took notice. Independent and student filmmakers added their wish lists. Before long, government agencies, event videographers, major networks and cable news outfits began placing orders. Sony introduced an entire line of DVCAM camcorders and VTR machines with an escalating list of features and costs. In five years, DVCAM has become the fastest growing format in Sony history.

DVCAM Tape and Cassettes

DVCAM Tape

There is an excellent section in John Nathan's book *Sony* about how Akio Morita, Masaru Ibuka and Nobutoshi Kihara developed magnetic tape and a tape recorder in 1950. They had read an old book on magnetism, which described how ferric oxide could be produced as a powder by heating oxalic ferrite. They found two jars at a pharmaceutical supplier. The chemical was then roasted in a borrowed frying pan, removed from the heat at just the right moment when the powder turned brown, and mixed with shellac. Rolls of smooth paper, strenghened with hemp, were cut by hand with two razor blades into quarter-inch-wide strips. Thirty-yard lengths of paper were then placed on the floor, and everyone went down on hands and knees, carefully painting the magnetic paste of oxide and shellac onto the paper using very expensive paint brushes made from the hair of badgers. When dry, the strips were wound onto small reels.

DVCAM tape today is almost the same width. However, fifty years has made quite a difference. It's also more correct to call it "media."

Both DVCAM and DV formats use Advanced Metal Evaporated tape. However, DVCAM tape costs a little more. It is manufactured on different machines to professional specifications. Materials are treated differently. The raw cobalt used as the magnetic medium is denser. The base film is more durable. DVCAM tape has 50% fewer dropouts, 50% less shrinkage and 25% increased resistance to wear. Its Diamond Like Carbon Coating (DLC) is optimized under more carefully controlled conditions. All these improvements over the DV format account for better picture, fewer artifacts, better carrier to noise ratio, less tape shrinkage over time, and longer tape life.

DVCAM tapes experience 50% fewer dropouts (those agonizing white streaks or dots in the picture, caused by loss of data), and have a better carrier-to-noise ratio (+2dB), which shows up as less grain in black areas, along with better image quality.

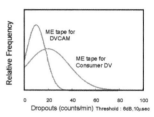

Distribution of dropouts of DVCAM and DVC tape

I didn't really believe all the differences until I saw the graphs and data, having previously wondered whether it was indeed some kind of marketing scheme or urban legend. The differences are real.

DVCAM tape uses Sony's Advanced Metal Evaporated (AME) technology. The entire process takes place in a vacuum. The magnetic layer is formed by evaporating ingots of cobalt. The resulting vapor of cobalt grain fuses directly to the base film, as a molecular bond, without binders or other additives.

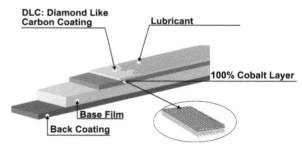

The tape surface is almost 100% magnetic material, which is why the recording tracks can be so thin—there is no need to worry whether the signal will travel across magnetic and non-magnetic areas. Because there is no binder (glue), the tape itself is smoother and thinner. The DLC layer improves durability; the lubricant reduces friction, jitter, and abrasion on the heads—and provides a more even tape speed. All of these attributes enable the cassette, in which the tape is housed, to be smaller. The tape is extremely clean running, and heads require less frequent cleaning.

Advanced Metal Evaporated technology takes magnetic tape to a new level, providing media with extremely short wavelength recording capabilities along with increased output. This means higher resolution, larger storage capacity, while keeping the physical size small. At the moment, a Standard DVCAM tape can hold 3 hours of recorded material, which amounts to about 34.5 GB of data. I suspect that AME Technology could be increased to over one terabyte per cassette within the next few years.

Speeds

DVCAM tape travels at 28.193mm/second (NTSC/60Hz) or 28.221 mm/sec (PAL/50Hz).

DV tape speed is 18.182 mm/second (NTSC/60Hz) or 18.831 mm/sec (PAL 50 Hz)

Either way, DVCAM tape travels about 1/3 faster than DV.

What plays back where

All DVCAM camcorders and VTRs can play back a tape recorded in the DV SP format.

The Master series of VTRs can play back DVCPRO (25Mbps) without the need for an adapter or changes to menu settings.

All DVCAM camcorders and VTRs record in DVCAM format.

Some DVCAM camcorders and VTRs are also able to record in DV SP mode (DSR-PD150, DSR-250, DSR-11, DSR-50).

Only the DSR-2000 plays back DV LP.

Comparing tape widths
DVCAM, DV and DVCPRO tape is 6.35 mm (¼ inch) wide, although it is usually referred to as 6mm tape.
Betacam, Digital Betacam, VHS and Betamax tape is ½ inch (12.7 mm) wide.
Hi8 and Video 8 tape is 8 mm (slightly less than 1/3 inch) wide.

Cassettes

There are two cassette sizes in the DVCAM and DV format: Mini and Standard. DVCPRO cassettes, which we'll talk about later, are included in the chart below for comparison:

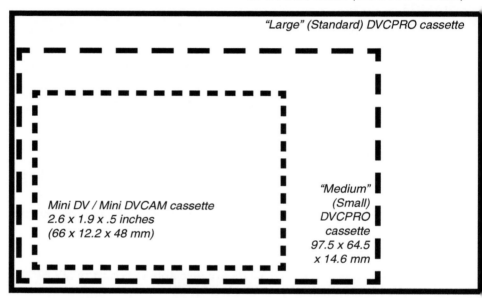

"Standard" (Large) DV / DVCAM cassette
4.9 x 3 x .57 inches (125 x 78 x 14.6 mm)

"Large" (Standard) DVCPRO cassette

Mini DV / Mini DVCAM cassette
2.6 x 1.9 x .5 inches
(66 x 12.2 x 48 mm)

"Medium"
(Small)
DVCPRO
cassette
97.5 x 64.5
x 14.6 mm

A large (Standard) size DVCAM cassette records up to 3 hours of video and audio. The small (Mini) DVCAM size records up to 40 minutes.

The "consumer" Mini DV cassette comes in 30 and 60 minute lengths.

You can squeeze 4½ hours of recording time onto a Standard DV cassette at the slow, LP speed, and 1.5 hours on the smaller Mini DV cassette, using a consumer DV camcorder. I don't recommend this. There is less margin for error; problems caused by tape stretching or handling might increase.

The Standard cassette is a little larger than a 1/8" audio or Video8 cassette. It fits in the bigger shoulder-resting cameras used by event videographers and news crews, and all VTRs. The large Sony camcorders will accept Mini cassettes without adapters. Of course, large cassettes cannot be used in small camcorders—yet.

The actual tape width is 6.35 mm (¼ inch) wide, and it moves at 18.81 mm/sec (0.75 inch/sec.) A 40-minute Mini DVCAM cassette uses about 233 feet (71 m) of tape. A 184-minute Standard DVCAM cassette has about 1,033 feet (315 m) of tape.

Cassette Memory

You can get cassettes with and without an integral memory chip, called "Cassette Memory" (CM). Cassettes containing the chip can be readily identified by their copper-colored band just below the **REC-SAVE** tab. The memory chip adds a small additional cost to each cassette, but provides the following benefits:

Date, title of tape, table of contents
Search tape by date of recording, searching tape by title or scene
Labeling a cassette, titles
Quickly finding the end of the last recorded scene

DVCAM cassettes store up to 16 Kilobits of data. DV cassettes can only hold up to 4 Kilobits.

Cassettes are available without the chips at a minor savings, but that's like buying the latest mountain bike with just one gear.

Recording DVCAM on consumer DV Cassettes

Emergency: middle of a shoot, can't find more DVCAM tapes. But the local Radio Shack has DV cassettes.

Consumer DV cassettes with 4 kilobits of IC memory, or without, can be used in DVCAM camcorders and decks.

Mini DV cassettes labeled for 60 minutes of DV recording can record up to 40 minutes of professional DVCAM in a DVCAM machine (multiply the DV time by 2/3 to get DVCAM time). The tape's not designed for professional use, and it will be lacking the 16 kilobit memory chip, but it will still work.

Recording DV on DV or DVCAM Cassettes

It is important to remember that you can record DV format on a DVCAM camcorder, using either kind of cassette. You must choose between DVCAM and DV formats when you set up your camcorder the first time— so be sure to choose DVCAM if you have a DVCAM machine.

Incidentally, if you use a DVCAM cassette in a DV-only camcorder, the resulting format will be DV. The hardware determines the format being recorded, not the cassette.

Comparison of Cassette sizes

The Mini DVCAM cassette measures 2.6 x 1.9 x .5 inches (66 x 48 x 12.2 mm).

In comparison, a Video 8 cassette is 3.7 x 2.5 x 0.6 inches (95 x 62.5 x 15 mm). A Mini DVCAM cassette takes up less than half the overall space (43.4%) of an 8 mm cassette.

A VHS cassette is 7.4 x 4.1 x .98 inches (188 x 104 x 25 mm).

Both the DVCAM and DV cassettes use a reel lock system to prevent tape sagging or unspooling.

Cassette Identification

DVCAM cassettes are identified by the DVCAM logo in the upper right. The lower left has a number, referring to minutes of recording time. ME stands for Metal Evaporated—the kind of tape used. A 32 minute Mini DVCAM cassette will read: "32 AdvancedME" on the tape cassette and "PDVM-32ME" on the cassette jacket. In this case, "ME" means Memory.

Mini DV cassettes have the Mini DV logo in the upper right. The number in the lower left identifies minutes of recording time.

So, a 30 minute Mini DV cassette will read: "DVM30." A two hour standard cassette will read: "DV 120." This labeling is the same whether the tape is for NTSC or PAL recording.

actual size MiniDV Cassette

Labeling Your Cassettes

After you finish shooting a cassette, slide the Safety Lock slider to the "SAVE" position. That prevents accidental re-recording over your once-in-a-lifetime shots.

To identify the tape, you'll have to do some origami tricks. Since the cassettes are so small, the adhesive labels on which you'll write scene information, date and contents are about the size of your thumbnail.

REC - SAVE = Record or Playback Only

Like other video formats and floppy disks, standard and Mini DVCAM cassettes have write-protect tabs.

REC is the position the slide switch must be in to enable recording onto tape.

SAVE is the position to save your work, preventing subsequent rerecording over it.

If you load a cassette whose slider is in the **SAVE** position, and the camcorder is in Standby, ready to record, you'll usually hear beeping noises, and an icon of a cassette with a line drawn through it will flash in the viewfinder.

These sliding "windows" are similar to those found in the Hi8 and Video8 formats—unlike the break-off tabs of the VHS cassette, the red button of U-matic, or the up-down tab of Betacam SP.

A DVCAM cassette shows an open hole to prevent recording, while a closed hole allows recording. This is similar to a 3½" computer floppy disk and a VHS cassette (open hole protects data, closed hole permits recording). The opposite scheme applies to Video/Hi8 (where an open hole allows recording).

Don't...Because

The cautions for handling digital video tape are pretty much the same as for any video or audio tape:

1.   Do not touch the tape itself. Oil from fingers can damage tape.

2.   Do not expose the tape to strong magnetic fields. That means: don't put the tape on top of a TV, monitor or speaker (they all emit magnetic fields), keep it away from magnetized screwdrivers, and of course, away from bulk tape erasers unless you really want to delete all contents.

3.   Try not to leave tapes in your car, especially in the sun.

4.   If the cassette is cold, let it warm up for at least 2 hours before using. Coming from cold outdoors to warm indoors, put the tape in a Zip-Lok plastic bag, and seal it tight. Any condensation formed in the warming process will cling to the outside of the bag, not the tape.

5.   When using tapes in hot, humid or dusty locations, store them in plastic bags, out of the sun.

6.   Do not leave the cassette in your camcorder for longer than necessary.

7.   Keep the cassette in its case, to protect it from dust and dirt.

8.   Tapes that are moist with humidity will shut down the equipment.

DVCAM Tape Online

Go to www.mediabysony.com for more information and a list of DVCAM tapes and places to buy them.

Replacement for U-matic?

For some strange reason, the advertising industry in this country relies on 3/4 inch U-matic tape to view samples of our work on a format dating back 30 years, and for which tape players are no longer even made. The cassettes are the size of this book, and twice as thick. Imagine how much money could be saved in shelf space, and the real estate rental to house those shelves, if ad agencies switched over to DVCAM tapes that are a fraction of the size, that last longer, and are much more versatile. The switch to DVCAM could finance the purchase of new players, with money left over.

A Guide to DVCAM

Let's begin by looking at DVCAM camcorders, deciding which one is particularly well suited to specific jobs, and learning the basics of how to use them.

Choosing a DVCAM Camcorder

You're a scientist on an expedition in the remotest jungle on earth. You have just discovered an aboriginal tribe, never before seen by the outside world. However, the cameraman recording your every move is doubled over in the canoe from the effects of last night's dinner, the bites of a dreadful insect, and the spell cast upon him by the local porters who think his camera has stolen their spirits. Your thoughts of Nobel rekindle early photography lessons in Boy Scouts. You grab the DSR-PD100A DVCAM from a soggy backpack.

Perhaps you are working on a student film. You are in charge of craft services—snacks and beverages. However, the producer thinks you are the Director of Photography, and hands you a DSR-PD150.

Your best friend's daughter is about to be married. The wedding videographer's DSR-250 DVCAM camcorder has just arrived. However, the videographer is stuck in traffic miles away.

You are the head of network news. You want to switch the entire department to DVCAM, and are trying to decide between the DSR-300A and DSR-500WS.

You shoot network news. Five minutes ago, they handed you a brand-new DSR-500WS to replace your venerable Betacam SP.

How do you choose which DVCAM camcorder is right for you?

And once you have a DVCAM camcorder, how do you figure out how to use it in ten minutes? You search in vain for the missing instruction manual.

About 230,000 DVCAM professional camcorders and VTRs have been sold worldwide so far. That means there should be 250,000 instruction manuals available. However, one of the immutable laws of production is that the appropriate instruction manual rarely travels with the intended camera, never makes it onto student productions, usually gets lost when you need it most, and takes too long to read.

The lightest and smallest of the professional DVCAM group is the DSR-PD100A. It has three 1/4" CCDs, a color viewfinder, flip-out LCD viewing screen, autofocus, image stabilization, and is about the size of many consumer palmcorders. It has a built-in microphone, along with an XLR input. Its small size makes it handy for sports and adventure projects.

Sony DSR-PD100A

Sony's DSR-PD150 is one of the most popular camcorders for corporate work, documentaries and student projects. It uses three 1/3" CCDs, has a black and white viewfinder, flip-out color LCD viewing screen, two XLR microphone inputs, autofocus, image stabilization and comes with a short shotgun mic.

Sony DSR-PD150

Next, we get to the shoulder-resting camcorders. Sony's DSR-250 accepts both Mini and Standard DVCAM cassettes for corporate projects, interviews, casting, events and weddings. It has the lens system, autofocus and image stabilization of the DSR-PD150, the black and white finder of its more expensive siblings, and a color LCD viewing screen.

Sony DSR-250

Sony's DSR-300A and DSR-500WS offer interchangeable lenses on a shoulder-resting camcorder. The DSR-300A has three 1/2" CCDs in 4:3 aspect ratio. The DSR-500WS has three 2/3" CCDs in a 16:9 shape, and offers the choice of 4:3 or 16:9 native formats. Beyond the chip size and a few minor details, both camcorders are similar.

Sony DSR-300

They share the black and white viewfinder of the DSR-250. Lenses attach to a bayonet mount. Audio controls are more advanced, as are timecode options and genlock connections. Setup files can be stored and recalled. Cliplink saves scene and logging information. There is no internal image stabilization or on-board LCD viewing screen.

Sony DSR-500

Sony DSR-PD100A

Sony's DSR-PD100A is the most affordable, easiest-to-learn entry point into the professional world of DVCAM. It is the quintessential "Handycam," sharing the familiar shape of the majority of consumer camcorders, along with an adjustable strap that presses your hand firmly against the body of the camera.

The DSR-PD100A is one of the smallest 3 CCD professional video camcorders that doesn't really look "professional." It looks like millions of other consumer Mini DV cameras, and bridges the gap between consumer, prosumer and larger professional models. A professional DVCAM camcorder disguised as a consumer body can be extremely useful when you don't want to call attention to yourself.

The DSR-PD100A accepts both DVCAM and Mini DV tape. The "A" means it is a newer model that replaces the DSR-PD100. It is the NTSC model; the PAL version is called DSR-PD100AP.

Sony's Consumer Division sells a camcorder that looks similar, the DCR-TRV900, that records only on Mini DV tape (not on DVCAM), lacks timecode and XLR audio input. Any one of these features is worth the slightly higher price of a DSR-PD100A, which further sweetens the deal with an included accessory wide-angle adaptor.

Three ¼" CCDs record 380,000 pixels interlaced (for video), or 480,000 progressive (for stills), capable of rendering an NTSC image of 500 horizontal TV lines. The minimum illumination is 4 lux. Most functions and camera status are displayed in the viewfinder. 480p (progressive as opposed to interlaced) is available for still images, or video at the equivalent of 15 fps.

The three CCDs in the DSR-PD100A are native 4:3, and aspect ratios are switchable from 4:3 to 16:9. The 4:3 format uses the entire chip, while 16:9 is created by recording in central horizontal area of the CCDs only.

The 12x zoom lens has Sony optics, auto and manual focus, and optical image stabilization. The lens is not removable, but many wide-angle and tele lens adapters are available, making interchangeable lenses less of an issue. An XLR adaptor mounts on top to connect either electret or dynamic microphones.

The viewfinder is color, and there is a swing-out 3.5" LCD display panel on the camera right side. Some people may prefer the black and white viewfinder of the next "higher" model, Sony's DSR-PD150. A black and white finder is sharper, which is helpful for critical determination of focus. A color finder has the advantage of being, well, color and truer to what is actually being recorded.

The camera has a built-in PCMCIA slot (PC Card) for Type II PC flash memory cards, and comes with a PCMCIA-to-Memory Stick adapter for still image storage. Up to 988 640x480 JPEG pictures (compressed 1/10) can be stored on one chewing-gum sized 64K Memory Stick, or 329 images at 1/3 compression. About 340 stills can be recorded on a 40-minute tape for 7 seconds each.

DSR-PD100A Camera Views

Front

Accessory hot shoe

52mm filter ring

Lens

Stereo microphone

Handgrip strap

IR remote control sensor

Rear

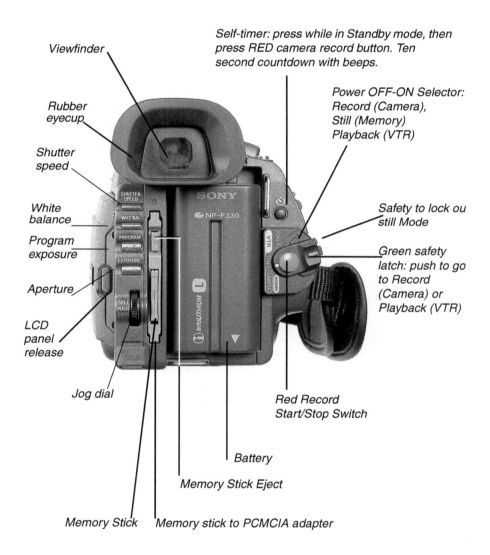

Self-timer: press while in Standby mode, then press RED camera record button. Ten second countdown with beeps.

Viewfinder

Power OFF-ON Selector: Record (Camera), Still (Memory) Playback (VTR)

Rubber eyecup

Shutter speed

White balance

Safety to lock ou still Mode

Program exposure

Green safety latch: push to go to Record (Camera) or Playback (VTR)

Aperture

LCD panel release

Jog dial

Red Record Start/Stop Switch

Battery

Memory Stick Eject

Memory Stick *Memory stick to PCMCIA adapter*

Top

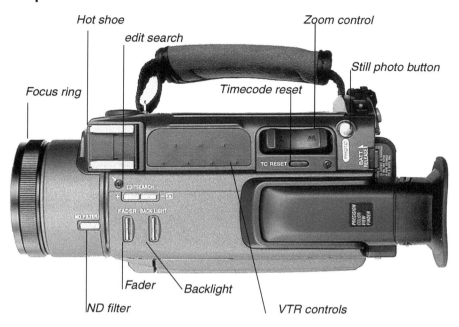

Hot shoe

edit search

Zoom control

Still photo button

Focus ring

Timecode reset

Fader

Backlight

ND filter

VTR controls

Bottom

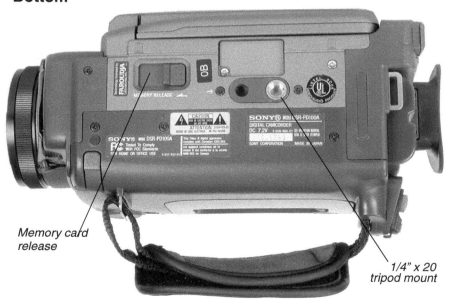

Memory card
release

1/4" x 20
tripod mount

Camera Left

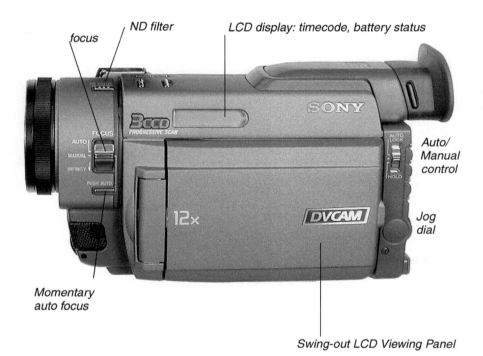

focus

ND filter

LCD display: timecode, battery status

Auto/
Manual
control

Jog
dial

Momentary
auto focus

Swing-out LCD Viewing Panel

Camera Right

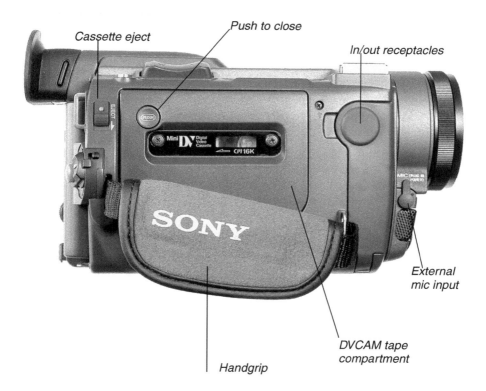

Cassette eject

Push to close

In/out receptacles

External
mic input

DVCAM tape
compartment

Handgrip

DSR-PD100A Jump Start

Removing Battery

The DSR-PD100A battery snaps onto the back of the camcorder, held in place by a push-button latch.

1. Lift up on the eyepiece to get it out of the way.

2. Press the **BATT RELEASE** (Battery Release) button—in the direction of its arrow.

3. It's easiest to use one hand: push the **Batt Release** button

with your index finger, and lift up on the battery with your thumb. Pull the battery away from the camera body.

Attaching Battery

To install a new battery, do the opposite.

1. Line up the top of the battery just below the **Batt Release** button.

2. Slide the battery toward the camera. (You'll see the **Batt Release** button being pushed in).

3 Push down until it locks in place with a click.

Recharging Battery

Plug the battery charger cable into the receptacle marked **DC IN** at the back of the camera.

Plug the power cord of the charger into a wall outlet. The charger is auto-sensing for 100 to 240 V AC. Charging time for the NP-F330 battery that comes with the camera is about 2.5 hours.

When charging is complete, the
battery/timecode display window
will read *FULL*. The time shown is
estimated battery life for recording
in minutes. (An NP-F330 battery
will last about 40 minutes. The
largest battery, NP-F960, takes
about 6.5 hours to charge, and will
last for about 4 hours of recording time.)

Loading Tape

To load the camera with tape, a
battery (or power supply) must be
connected. However, you do NOT
have to turn the camera on.

1. To open the tape cover, press
    the little blue button and, at the
    same time, push the **EJECT**
    button in the direction of its
    arrow.

2. The spring-loaded door is
    released by a servo, and pops
    open. Note: If the handgrip strap
    is too tight, it may prevent the
    tape door from fully opening.
    Load a Mini DVCAM or Mini DV
    cassette into the tray.

3. The clear window on the
    cassette, which shows tape
    remaining, faces out. Be sure the
    REC - SAVE slider on the bottom
    of the cassette is set to the Record

position. If it is in the SAVE position, you will see a flashing tape icon with
a slash through it, telling you the camera cannot record on the tape.

4. Slide the cassette all the way
    down into the chamber. Close the
    tape cover by pushing on the
    button labelled "**PUSH.**" If you
    don't push on **PUSH**, the cover
    probably will not latch closed.

Shooting: Quick Start

This is the emergency section. You just pulled the camera out of its case, and you have to shoot in a hurry. Here's a quick checklist on default settings and auto-everything.

1. I'm embarrassed to say it, but remove the lens cap.

2. The camera's Main Power Switch has 4 positions: **CAMERA** (to record), **MEMORY** (still pictures), **OFF**, and **VTR** (playback).

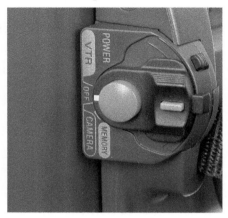

(The green button in the center of the Main Power Switch is a safety latch to help prevent accidental changes.)

3. But first, there's another safety slider that can actually make things a lot easier. The little, un-labelled slide switch lurking at 2 o'clock— above and to the right of the Main Switch—can help prevent accidentally going into Still Photo Mode when you really want to be shooting Video. Slide the switch toward the rear of the camera to LOCK OUT Still Photo Mode.

4. Push the little green bar in with your thumb, and move the 4-position lever to the **CAMERA** position. You are ready to shoot. The camera is in the sublime state of readiness called "Standby," indicated by the abbreviation **STBY** in the viewfinder.

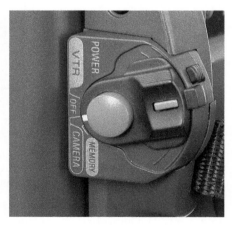

5. Press the red button once to begin recording. You'll see **REC** for "Record" in the viewfinder. Press again to stop tape. Press again to resume shooting. And so on.

6. Turn the Main Power Switch **OFF** when you want to conserve power. If the camera stays in standby more than five minutes, it turns off by itself.

Auto Everything

The most beautiful stampede of zebras the world has ever seen is taking place right in front of you. No time to read the rest of this manual, nor to fumble with the other kind of manual—the manual settings you painstakingly entered last night for that low-light animals-in-the-watering-hole sequence illuminated by vehicle headlamps. If you use the same exposure settings now, you'll be about 20 stops over-exposed.

Auto Lock and Auto Focus

On the camera left side, set the **AUTO LOCK—HOLD** switch to the top (**AUTO LOCK**) position.

This setting basically "locks" out manual settings, and lets the camera automatically set exposure, shutter speed, and white balance.

Set the **FOCUS** switch to **AUTO**.

Viewfinder Warnings

Check the viewfinder, and if you see the following warnings, push the appropriate switch until the warning disappears:

ND ON—press the **ND FILTER** switch to activate the ND filter (cut down light).

ND OFF—press the **ND FILTER** switch to allow more light through the lens.

Square with quarter sun icon — press the **BACK LIGHT** switch.

FADER, MONOTONE, OVERLAP— press the **FADER** switch.

Eyepiece and Eyecup

The viewfinder contains optics that magnify the image displayed on a small internal color LCD screen. You can set the correct diopter for your eyesight by moving the adjustment lever until the letters displayed in the viewfinder are sharpest. (This is easier and more accurate than focusing the diopter on a distant object).

Handgrip

Do not carry the camera by its eyepiece or the microphone. Use the handgrip.

When handholding, the strap should be snug against the back of your hand. Lift up the velcro cover with the SONY logo, and tighten the strap.

Lens and Sunshade

The included sunshade screws onto the lens. Line up the locating pin at 3 o'clock on the lens with its matching indentation on the sunshade.

locating pin

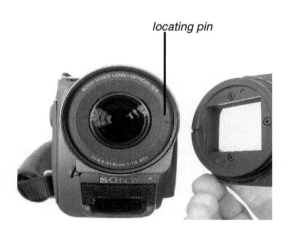

LCD Viewing Screen

To open the LCD monitor, press the silver OPEN button, and swing the monitor panel out.

The viewfinder shuts off when the LCD screen is out, except in mirror mode.

LCD panel tilts up and down, and flips over 180 degrees into mirror mode for narcissistic self portraiture.

LCD brightness ➡

Volume control for monitor speaker ➡

LCD panel swings out up to 90 degrees from camera body

ND Filter

When you see the words "ND ON" flashing in the viewfinder or on the LCD screen, the scene is very bright, and the camera suggests you activate the internal Neutral Density filter. It's like sunglasses for the video pickup chips. The ND filter is actually a piece of optical glass tinted gray.

When the words "ND OFF" flash in the viewfinder, the camera is telling you it needs more light. Press the **ND FILTER** switch on top of the camera near the lens.

Manual Exposure

When the action is slower and less controlling of your destiny than, for example, racing with the bulls of Pamplona, controlling manual exposure will yield better pictures.

AUTO LOCK Switch Off

Turn off the camera's autopilot by sliding the **AUTO LOCK** switch to its middle position.

The center position is Manual Control, should be labeled as such, and probably would have been if there were room to say Manual Control of Exposure, Shutter, White Balance and other things.

The bottom position is **HOLD**, where you can lock in your manual settings. This switch is useful to compare automatic and manual exposure settings.

You can switch out of Auto, set a manual exposure, as described next, and then flip back and forth with this switch between the two modes.

When you're shooting an independent feature or a job that requires careful matching from scene to scene, use the manual settings by sliding the **AUTO LOCK** switch to the middle position.

Enable all of the following by pushing the respective buttons: **GAIN, SHUTTER SPEED, WHITE BALANCE** and **IRIS**.

To change a manual setting, push the appropriate button (it will change from white to black in the viewfinder) and adjust with the jog wheel. Try shooting with 0 dB gain and at 1/60th second shutter speed, which will be displayed as "60" in the viewfinder.

Setting EXPOSURE (Aperture)

1. Press the **EXPOSURE** button on the back of the camera to turn manual exposure on.

A linear scale appears in the upper left corner of the eyepiece or LCD screen. The minus sign means darker (closing down the iris), the plus sign means brighter (opening the iris).

The actual F stop is displayed in the finder in 1/2 stop increments at the lower left of the display.

2. Turn the control dial up or down to adjust the F stop. Pushing in on the control dial will have no effect. To lock it in, slide the **AUTO LOCK** switch to **HOLD**.

The aperture is adjustable from F2 to F11. Closing down further than F11 shuts out all light, as indicated by CLOSE in the finder. Opening wider than F2 kicks in electronic gain, indicated in 3 dB increments up to +18 dB. Electronic gain introduces grain, or "noise," to the picture.

There are no click stops for the aperture settings, nor are there end stops for the dial.

Backlight

There is a **BACKLIGHT** button on top of the camera. It only works in **AUTO LOCK** mode. It's a quick way to open the aperture about a stop when a backlit subject looks too dark against a bright background. For example, when you're shooting a close-up of your daughter on the ski slope, the ambient brightness of the snow fools the camera into thinking the whole scene is the brightness of snow. So your little darling's face will be too dark. Press the **BACKLIGHT** button to brighten her up. Better yet, use manual exposure control.

Shutter

With the **AUTO LOCK** switch in its center, manual position, you can adjust the shutter speed of the camera from 1/4 to 1/10,000 second (1/3 to 1/10,000 on PAL model).

1. Press the **SHUTTER SPEED** button on the back of the camera.

2. Turn the control dial.

3. The shutter speed will be displayed at the lower left of the viewfinder or LCD screen.

High shutter speeds are useful for freezing quickly moving action either as still frames or in post production. Remember, you're still shooting at 30 images per second (25 in PAL), so it's not slow motion; you are simply capturing each one of those images in a much shorter span of time. There can be a few disadvantages to fast shutter speeds—similar to the ones encountered when using a motion picture camera. Vertical objects may strobe when panning, and car wheels sometimes look like they are turning the wrong way.

Slow shutter speeds

Slow shutter speeds of 1/4 and 1/8 second provide a smeared, semi-slow motion look similar to filming at 6 frames per second and transferring that footage to video at 6 frames per second. In essence, the camera is recording the same image for a duration of 1/4 second, smearing it electronically with motion blur, and then recording the next image for 1/4 second. So, in one second, you get about 6 discreet images.

Program AE

Programmed Auto Exposure is a carry-over from the world of still photography. You probably will not use it very often, but sometimes it can be very useful.

1. With the **AUTO LOCK** in the middle position, push the **PROGRAM AE** switch at the rear of the camera.

2. Spin the jog control dial to one of five exposure settings. You will see an icon at the lower left of the viewfinder or LCD display: Aperture Priority, Shutter Priority, Sports Lesson, Sunset and Moon, and Low Lux.

3. **A** and **S** indicate Aperture Priority and Shutter Priority. To select either one, push in on the control dial, and then rotate the control dial to select either your aperture or shutter speed. Push the control dial again to lock in the setting.

Aperture Priority

In Aperture Priority, you pick an aperture from F1.6 to F11. The camera automatically selects the correct shutter speed, and will boost gain if there still is not enough light. Aperture Priority is useful when you want to shoot with minimum depth of field—meaning that almost everything except your subject will be out of focus. The wider open the lens (F1.6), the less depth of field. Shallow depth of field overcomes video's drawback of having too much in focus, which makes things look "flat." Note that the lens is not as fast in telephoto as it is in wide angle. The widest you'll be able to open at 51.6mm is F2.8, while at 4.3mm, you can open all the way to F1.6. This is inherent to the design of the lens. Having a uniform aperture throughout the zoom range would make the lens much bigger and heavier.

Shutter Priority

In Shutter Priority, you select a shutter speed from 1/60 to 1/10,000 of a second (1/50 to 1/10,000 in PAL), and the camera sets the aperture (and ND filtration).

Sports Lesson Mode

The fast shutter speeds of sports lesson mode help to sharpen motion blur, and are useful for reviewing the tape frame by frame later on. Imagine recording your daughter's tennis serve. At normal speed, the camcorder captures each frame at 1/60th second. The tennis ball will be blurred, because 1/60th second is an eternity for a moving tennis ball. But if we record each frame at 1/10,000th second, the tennis ball in each frame will be frozen with detailed clarity. This is great for tennis and baseballs, but if you record someone running, the effect when played back might be jittery.

Sunset and Moon

This should actually be called Magic Hour Mode, or Dusk Exposure. Magic Hour is the time between the dark and the daylight, when the night is beginning to lower—and the light is great for shooting cars, landscapes, and architecture against glowing skies. Clients, producers and agency folks would much prefer to forego the overtime usually incurred by their crews chasing around after sunset instead of safely ensconced at the bar enjoying Happy Hour instead of Magic Hour. In Magic Hour Mode, the camera compensates for dark backgrounds behind point sources of light. It's good for neon signs, fireworks, sunsets, buildings lit at night—all those situations where there are points of light that would otherwise be washed out if the camera based its exposure on the overall dark scene.

Low Lux

Low lux lets even more light into the camera than Magic Hour Mode. The shutter speed becomes slow, and you get an interesting, slightly blurred and jittery look if you're panning. This is not quite night vision—but you can shoot in some pretty dark places without too much grain or noise from gain boosts.

Focus, Zoom, Zebra Stripes, etc.

Focus, Zoom, Zebra Stripes, Gain, ND, Timelapse and other things will be covered later. See "Common Features: All Models" beginning page 129.

Menu and Navigation

Nokia gets my award for best digital menus. Nokia cell phones have the most logical layout and the best menu structure, which make navigation a breeze. They use "soft keys," which are simply buttons whose identification labels show up on the LCD screen. To save space, reduce clutter and use fewer buttons, the function that each button performs can change from time to time. However, it is still consistent and logical, and always clearly labeled.

The worst digital menus are the ones on your VCR or fax machine. A six-year-old, and most adults, can figure out Nokia's text-driven soft keys and up-down buttons. I urge all engineers to seriously look at a Nokia cell phone before designing their menus.

The menu, mode and dial system on Sony's DSR-PD100A isn't bad, but you won't praise its virtues, either, when you have to quickly change settings during that spectacular takeoff of five thousand flamingoes against the blood-orange setting sun.

To use the menu, press **MENU**

Turn the jog wheel to navigate.

Press in on the jog wheel to accept a choice.

The jog dial on this camcorder makes navigation much easier than on most other cameras, but I still live in the hopes of a return to the simpler analog dials and switches for dedicated functions that we are mercifully returning to still cameras like the Nikon F4 and F5.

CAMERA Menu

When the Main Power Switch is set to
CAMERA,

you have the following choices when you push
the **MENU** button:

(note—default values are shown first)

(my recommendations starred)

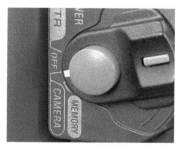

MANUAL SET -   AUTO SHUTTER - ON */ OFF
                        PROGRESSIVE SCAN - OFF */ ON
CAMERA SET -   DIGITAL ZOOM - OFF */ ON
                        16:9 - OFF */ ON
                        STEADYSHOT - ON */OFF
                        AE SHIFT -   - *set with jog dial*
                        GAIN SHIFT - 0dB */ -3 dB
                        FRAME REC - OFF / ON
                        INTERVAL RECORD - OFF / ON
                        RETURN
LCD / VIEWFINDER SET - LCD BACKLIGHT - BRIGHT / NORMAL
                                    (only with battery)
                        LCD COLOR   - set with jog dial
                        VIEWFINDER BRIGHTNESS - set with jog dial
                        RETURN
CASSETTE MEMORY SET - TITLE ERASE
                        TAPE TITLE - set with jog dial
                        ERASE ALL - RETURN / ok
                        RETURN
TAPE SET -   AUDIO MODE - 32k / 48k *
                        MIC LEVEL - AUTO */ MANUAL use jog dial
                        TAPE REMAINING - AUTO */ ALWAYS ON
                        TIME CODE - DF / NDF (NON DROP FRAME) *
SETUP MENU-   CLOCK SET - set with jog dial
                        LETTER SIZE - NORMAL / 2x
OTHERS -   WORLD TIME (time zone adjustment)
                        BEEP - MELODY / NORMAL / OFF
                        COMMANDER (remote) - ON / OFF
                        DISPLAY - LCD / V-OUT+LCD
                        REC LAMP - ON / OFF
                        COLOR BAR - OFF / ON
                        RETURN

MEMORY Menu

When the Main Power Switch is set to **MEMORY**
for shooting stills, you have the following choices
when you push the **MENU** button:

MANUAL SET
CAMERA SET
LCD / VF SET
MEMORY SET-CONTINUOUS - OFF / ON / MULTI SCREEN
        QUALITY - STANDARD / FINE / SUPER FINE
        PROTECT - OFF / ON
        SLIDE SHOW -
        DELETE ALL - RETURN / OK
        FORMAT   RETURN / OK
        RETURN
SETUP MENU
ETC

VTR Menu

When the Main Power Switch is set to **VTR**,
you have the following choices when you push the
MENU button:

VTR SET - HI FI SOUND - STEREO / 1 (LEFT TRACK) 2 (RIGHT TRACK)
        AUDIO MIX (BALANCE)
        LCD / VF SET
        MEMORY SET
        CASSETTE MEMORY SETcm search - ON / OFF
                TITLE ERASE
                TITLE DISPLAY - ON / OFF
                TAPE TITLE
                ERASE ALL
                RETURN
      TAPE SET
      SETUP MENU
      OTHERS   BEEP
                  COMMANDER
                  DISPLAY
                  DV EDITING
                  RETURN

DSR-PD150

Overview

Honey, they shrank the camcorder. Sony's DSR-PD150 looks like a professional news camera shrunk down to Handycam size. It's the darling of independent filmmakers, local news stations, documentarians and just about anyone else looking for the most quality in the smallest body.

This is one of the hottest camcorders on the market. Why?

The image is exceptionally sharp and the circuits have an uncanny ability to control contrast, keeping impossible highlights from burning out while retaining shadow detail.

The silky-smooth electric zoom has an equally smooth manual control on the barrel.

A handle on top facilitates low-angle shots, and easy-access buttons enable manual control of iris and audio levels.

For a Few Dollars More

The DSR-PD150 shares some of the same features as Sony consumer division's DCR-VX2000, and is made in the same factory. So what do we get for an extra fistful of about $1,000?

DSR-PD150

For that matter, why should we spend the extra bucks for a DSR-PD150 instead of a DSR-PD100A?

Three 1/3" CCDs

DCR-VX2000

The DSR-PD150 has three 1/3" CCDs with 380,000 pixels each (effectively 340,000 pixels), while the DSR-PD150P (PAL) has three 1/3-inch CCDs with 450,000 pixels (effectively 400,000 pixels).

The three chips of the DSR-PD150 are larger than on the DSR-PD100A (1/3" vs 1/4"). These CCDs are capable of both interlace scan for motion and progressive scan for stills.

200,000 Dot 2.5" Color LCD Monitor

The DSR-PD150 has a high-resolution color LCD monitor that is bright even outdoors and in snow. The 2.5" color LCD viewing screen is slightly smaller than the DSR-PD100A's 3.5" screen, but it seems to be brighter.

180,000 Dot LCD Black &White Viewfinder

The black and white viewfinder provides 500 lines of horizontal resolution—more than 20% greater than current color viewfinders. This helps manual focusing. Although it's a matter of personal taste, I find the DSR-PD150's black-and-white finder to be sharper, especially for critical focus, than the color viewfinder of the DSR-PD100A, or the consumer version DCR-VX2000.

DSR-PD150 — 2 ch XLR Audio Input

There are two XLR receptacles (on the camera right side in front of the carrying handle) for audio input and connecting professional microphones. The input level can be selected from Mic/Line/Mic Attenuator positions. INPUT 1 audio can be recorded on either CH1, or CH1 and CH2 audio tracks (selected by switch).

The two XLR audio inputs have switches to provide 48 volt phantom powering for professional microphones. The consumer DCR-VX2000 has a single RCA unbalanced audio input, and the DSR-PD100A has a single, unpowered XLR receptacle.

The dual, balanced, phantom-powered XLR inputs and controls more than justify the extra cost of admission. You can buy aftermarket mixers and mic power sources for your DCR-VX2000, but you'll wind up spending almost the same amount. The mini shotgun mic of the DSR-PD150 is easily detached from its shock mount; the DCR-VX2000's mic is permanently attached. The supplied ECM-NV1 mini shotgun microphone provides good sound, and the removable shock mount isolates the camcorder's motor noise.

16-bit/12-bit PCM Digital Sound and Audio Dub Capability

The DSR-PD150 records two channels of audio in the 48kHz/16-bit setting or four channels in the 32kHz/12-bit mode. On a pre-recorded tape with two channels recorded in the 32kHz/12-bit mode, it can dub two additional channels through the external mic input (XLR connectors or RCA receptacles, DVCAM tape only).

Timecode Options

The timecode can be preset using any number in Hour/Minute/Second/Frame format, and offers the choice of "record-run" or "free run." User bits can also be set. This is a big bonus for such a little camera, allowing you to identify each tape. In contrast, the DSR-PD100A can only reset timecode to 0.

12x Zoom Lens

The Sony optics 12x lens is threaded for 58 mm filters. The lens is not interchangeable—it is permanently mounted to the camera body, which of course, saves size and weight. An optical image stabilizer, in which the horizontal and vertical movements are detected independently by electronic sensors, activates a prism system located at the front of the lens to adjust and optically compensate for unsteadiness.

The DSR-PD150 lens zooms in farther than the DSR-PD100A (6-72mm vs 4.3-51mm), is slightly faster (f2.4 vs f2.6) and is optically slightly better. Mechanically, the lens is one of the smoothest of any small camcorder, with a dampening mechanism that feathers the end stops of the zoom.

Manual focus is an easy switch from **AUTO**. The handle on top is very helpful for carrying and low-angle shots.

DVCAM/DV Recording

The DSR-PD150 is a DVCAM camcorder. However, it is also capable of recording and playing back DV format tapes (SP mode only), which can be useful when you've run out of DVCAM tape and the only store within 400 miles carries DV tapes only. You select the format from the menu.

Power

The DSR-PD150 uses 7.2 volt Lithium Ion batteries. The power consumption is 4.7 W (with viewfinder). With an optional NP-F960 battery pack, you can record for up to eight hours.

Digital Still Camera Functions with Memory Stick

Still images can be recorded directly to DVCAM tape or to a Memory Stick, which is inserted directly into the back of the DSR-PD150.

Progessive Scan Still Photos

The camera can be switched to the progressive scan mode for capturing still images. VGA-sized (640x480) JPEG files are recorded on the Memory Stick in one of three image quality modes.

Accidental Tourists

This is about as good as it gets for ultra-portable DVCAM. It shares many of the same features as its larger sibling, the DSR-250. The notable difference is that the DSR-250 accepts larger DVCAM cassettes as well as Mini.

The main difference between this camera and the larger DSR-300A and DSR-500WS professional cameras is that these bigger brothers use interchangeable lenses, have 1/2" or 2/3" chips, and also accept large size DVCAM cassettes. However, the DSR-300A and 500WS look serious when you're trying to be inconspicuous. When you would rather look like a tourist, a much smaller camcorder like the DSR-PD150 makes a reliable companion.

DSR-PD150 Camera Views

Front

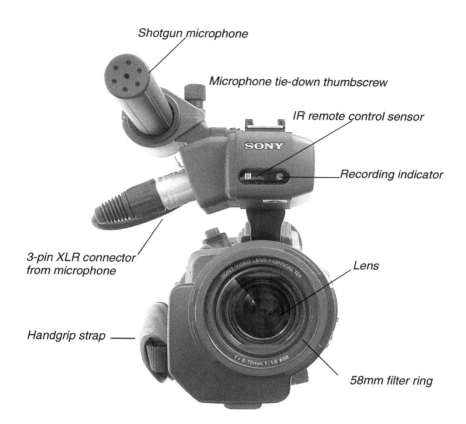

Shotgun microphone

Microphone tie-down thumbscrew

IR remote control sensor

Recording indicator

3-pin XLR connector from microphone

Lens

Handgrip strap

58mm filter ring

Rear

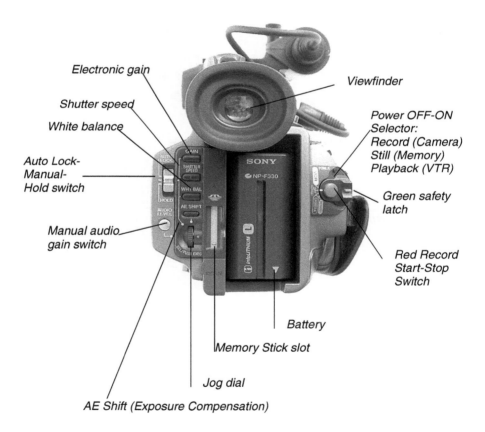

Electronic gain

Shutter speed

White balance

Auto Lock-
Manual-
Hold switch

Manual audio
gain switch

AE Shift (Exposure Compensation)

Jog dial

Memory Stick slot

Battery

Viewfinder

Power OFF-ON
Selector:
Record (Camera)
Still (Memory)
Playback (VTR)

Green safety
latch

Red Record
Start-Stop
Switch

Top

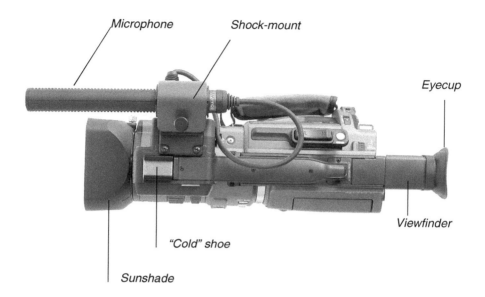

Microphone   Shock-mount

Eyecup

Viewfinder

"Cold" shoe

Sunshade

Bottom

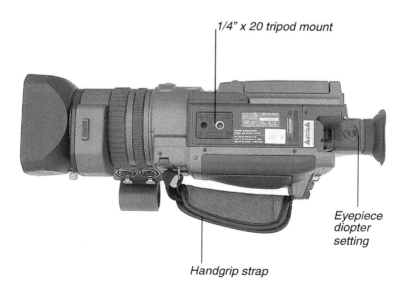

1/4" x 20 tripod mount

Eyepiece diopter setting

Handgrip strap

Camera Left

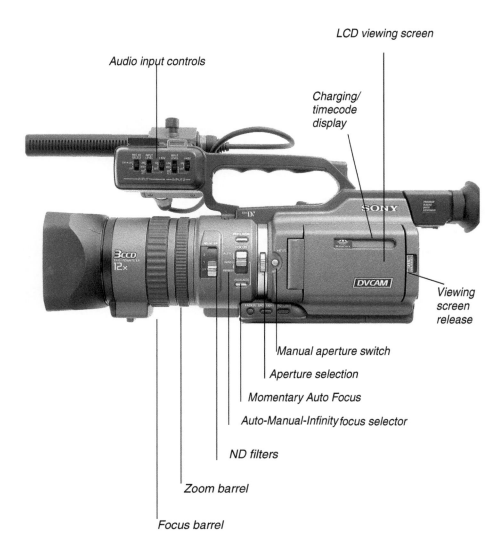

LCD viewing screen

Audio input controls

Charging/
timecode
display

Viewing
screen
release

Manual aperture switch

Aperture selection

Momentary Auto Focus

Auto-Manual-Infinity focus selector

ND filters

Zoom barrel

Focus barrel

Camera Right

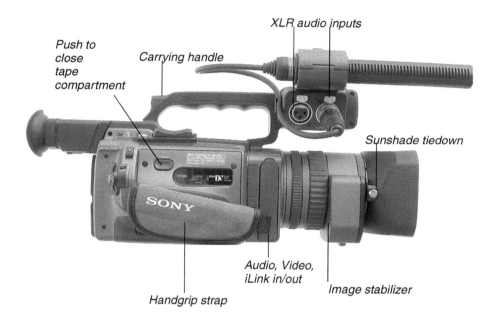

Push to
close
tape
compartment

Carrying handle

XLR audio inputs

Sunshade tiedown

Audio, Video,
iLink in/out

Image stabilizer

Handgrip strap

DSR-PD150 Jump Start

Attach the Battery

I hope readers will forgive me for beginning with a task almost as obvious as the admonition not to carry the camera by its eyepiece, but we have to assume the mythical World's Worst Cameraman is reading this.

1. Lift the viewfinder out of the way

2. Hold the battery so the SONY logo is on top, and the small arrow faces down.

3. Suggestion: hold the battery in your left hand—left thumb above the "S" in SONY, left index finger below the "i" of infoLITHIUM.

4. Slide the top of the battery along the top of battery compartment until it stops.

5. Then, push the battery down until you hear a click.

How to Detach the Battery

To remove the battery, press the **BATT RELEASE** button.

Lift up on the battery, and then pull it away from the camera.

Attach the Microphone

When you first unpack the DSR-PD150 from its box, you may notice the mic is not attached.

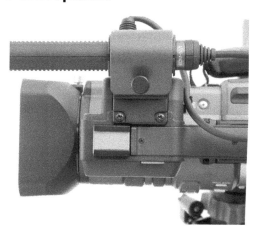

I failed to realize this the first time I used the camcorder, and imagine my surprise at not being able to record sound.

Of course, the Sony instruction manual clearly tells you how—but who reads instructions?

1. Loosen the thumbscrew on top of the microphone shock mount.

2. Open the mount.

3. Rest the mic inside so the slit in its rubber sleeve faces up. "ECM-NV1" faces up.

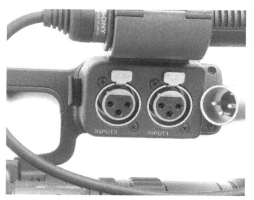

4. Tighten the mount—finger tight.

5. Plug the 3-pin XLR microphone connector into **INPUT 1.**

6. There's a little cord clip to keep the cable out of your way.

When it's time to unplug the XLR connector, push in on the silver-colored tab before yanking the plug out.

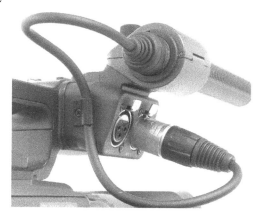

Set the Microphone Controls

There are 5 switches that must be set for the audio to work. Here are my suggestions when using just the on-board shotgun mic.

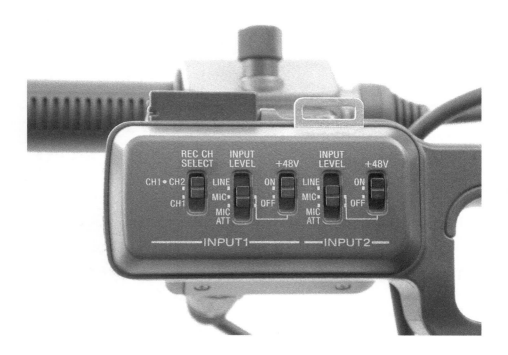

Working left to right, the first three switches control the mic plugged into **INPUT 1**:

1. Set **REC CH SELECT** (Record Channel Select) to **CH1-CH2**. This means that even though you have plugged the mic into **INPUT 1**, the audio is being recorded on two tracks of the DVCAM tape.

2. Set **INPUT LEVEL** to **MIC**. Line would be for recording from a CD player or other line source. **MIC ATT** means Microphone Attenuated. That would make the audio recording about 20dB lower, or softer, than the regular **MIC** position. You might use **MIC ATT** at a rock concert or kindergarten class.

3. Set **+48V** to **ON**. Many professional microphones require low amperage, 48 volt external power. The ECM-NV1 that comes with the DSR-PD150 requires phantom powering. If you're not sure what kind of mic you have, try it first with phantom powering off. If there's no audio, then turn it on.

4, 5. Doesn't matter with one mic. These switches control a mic plugged into **INPUT 2**, which we haven't done.

Windscreen

Use the foam windscreen outdoors. Indoors, it's not really necessary.

Microphone Mounting further Aft

Sometimes it's a little cumbersome packing the camera with its microphone protruding in front of the lens, especially if you're carrying the DSR-PD150 in a padded backpack or small case.

Although purists might shudder at the thought of covering up some of the side baffles of the mini shotgun mic, I can't really hear much difference.

A rubber sleeve is attached at the factory to the ECM-NV1 mic, using clear double-sided tape. This prevents the rubber sleeve from getting lost.

If you want to have a second mounting position for the mic, gently peel the rubber sleeve from the mic, and re-position it midway. Use a rubber band to prevent losing it.

Load Tape

1. You can load tape with the camcorder's Main Power Switch in any position.

Press the blue Eject button while sliding the **EJECT** switch in the direction of the arrow.

2. If the handgrip strap is too tight, it may prevent the cassette lid from fully opening. Loosen the strap by separating the velcro sections apart.

3. After the cassette tray below the lid is opened by its servo motor, insert a DVCAM cassette. (The SONY logo should be facing you, upside-down.)

4. Press the **PUSH** button on the lid until it clicks closed.

Power On

Turn the Main Power Switch to the **CAMERA** position.

It's a good idea to slide the **LOCK** safety switch in the direction of the arrow to prevent taking stills when you really wanted to record motion.

1. When you first power up the camcorder, a "welcome" screen is displayed against a black viewfinder background (blue background if you are looking at the LCD viewing panel. InfoLITHIUM is the rechargeable lithium ion battery designed for the DSR-PD100A and DSR-PD150.

2. About a second later, you'll see this screen if a tape is loaded.

It shows, clockwise, from 12 o'clock: **CM** (most DVCAM cassettes have an internal chip, Cassette Memory); **STBY** (Camera is Standing By); Timecode; Tape remaining in minutes (31 minutes in this example); **DVCAM** recording mode; and **48K** audio recording mode.

If no tape is loaded, a cassette icon with a line will flash center screen.

3. After another second or two, you should see picture (here, we just see the back of the lens cap). To make the on-screen information disappear, open the LCD viewing screen, and push the **DISPLAY** button.

4. Warning: if the Date and Time remain on screen, they will be indelibly recorded on tape. You probably want to turn it off. Read on.

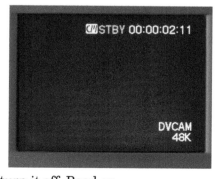

External Power and Charging

If you just unpacked your camcorder, the battery needs to be charged. Turn the Main Power Switch to **OFF (CHG)**.

Lift the rubber **DC IN** flap, and plug the charger cable in. The embossed +- ID at the end of the charger cable faces the camcorder's battery.

You can operate the camcorder while charging.

If you find the camcorder does not work, most likely the charger's plug has been kicked out of the wall outlet. The battery will not supply power to the camera if the charger/AC power source is connected.

The NP-F330 battery, that comes with the camera, takes about 2.5 hours to charge.

The LCD timecode/battery status display (on the camera left side) shows how much recording time the battery can provide. When charging is completed, it will read **FULL**.

Because it is designed to provide information on remaining power and state of charge, it's not a good idea to use home-made or improvised electric screwdriver Nicad cells.

DSR-PD150 Battery Life

Continuous Recording Time, indoors at 25 °C

Battery	with Viewfinder	with LCD Monitor on
NP-F330 (supplied)	60 min.	50 min.
NP-F550	130 min.	110 min.
NP-F750	265 min.	230 min.
NP-F960	480 min.	420 min.

Sunshade and Lens Cap

There are a few more things to do: some obvious, some not.

Attach the sunshade by aligning the index marks.

Tighten the knurled knob.

There's a handy little leash on the lens cap to attach it to the camera. Although the leash prevents losing the cap, I prefer not having it dangling and bouncing around in the middle of a shot. It usually is attached to the handgrip strap—but draping the lenscap leash over the mic makes it a lot easier to remove.

DSR-PD150 Auto-Every-thing Settings

At the rear of the camera, check that the **AUTO LOCK-HOLD** switch is set to the **AUTO LOCK** (top) position. Auto Lock disables manual settings of Gain, Shutter Speed, White Balance and Iris that you might have been set previously.

In the picture at right, the **AUTO LOCK** switch is in the Manual (middle) position.

HOLD (the bottom position) holds, or "remembers" all your manual settings, and prevents accidentally changing them.

On the camera left side, check that the **FOCUS** switch is set to the **AUTO** (top) position.

Slide the **ND FILTER** switch to **OFF**.

DSR-PD150 Manual Settings

When you're shooting an independent feature or a job that requires careful matching from scene to scene, use the manual settings by sliding the **AUTO LOCK** switch to the middle position.

Enable all of the following by pushing the respective buttons: **GAIN, SHUTTER SPEED, WHITE BALANCE** and **IRIS**.

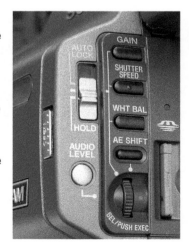

To change a manual setting, push the appropriate button (it will change from white to black in the viewfinder) and adjust with the jog wheel. Try shooting with 0 dB gain and at 1/60th second shutter speed, which will be displayed as "60" in the viewfinder.

Menu Selections

You have one final pre-flight checklist: reviewing the menu settings. Open the LCD viewing screen panel by pushing the silver **OPEN** button at the rear of the camera.

The LCD panel pivots 90° out from the camera body, and spins 270°.

Adjust the Brightness of the LCD Viewing Screen with the push-button switches on the left.

Volume is for playing back audio on the internal speaker.

The Main Power Switch at the back of the camcorder should be in the **CAMERA** position.

Push the **MENU** button.

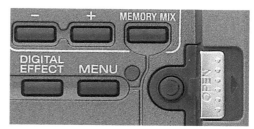

Rotate the **SEL/PUSH EXEC** jog dial at the rear of the camera to *change* selections. Push in on the jog dial to *make* a selection.

Let's illustrate the process of choosing from the menu by looking at how to set timecode, which has more choices on the DSR-PD150 than the DSR-PD100A.

After that is a brief rundown of some suggestions for important menu settings.

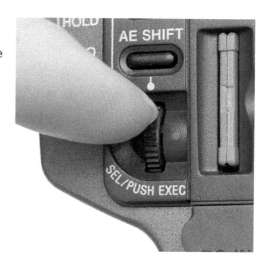

Timecode Menu

This is the Menu Home Page. You get here when you push the **MENU** button.

It is divided into two columns.

The column on the left shows icons of the main choices you can make.

The column on the right is headed by an explanation of the icon, under which are the choices that can be made.

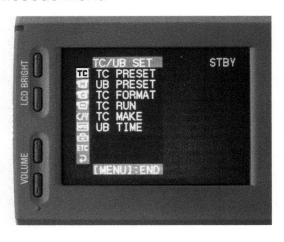

TC/UB SET (Timecode/User Bits) is highlighted when you first push the MENU button.

When you rotate the jog dial, the icon selected is identified at the top of the right-hand column.

There are a lot of choices, and they don't all fit intuitively under the eight categories—but neither do the menu choices in Microsoft Word or Adobe Photoshop. As I've mentioned before, I think the only menus that have achieved the nirvana where everything fits perfectly and logically exist on Nokia cell phones.

Nevertheless, the choices on the DSR-PD150 are not daunting, and it's a good idea to explore them all.

The main column of icons lets you choose:

TC Timecode (timecode, user bits, timecode format, etc.)

M Manual Settings (shutter, scan mode, black level)

Camera Settings (digital zoom, 16:9/4:3, SteadyShot, timelapse, etc.)

LCD/VF Settings (LCD screen and viewfinder options)

CM CM Settings (cassette memory functions like title, erase, etc.)

TAPE Settings (DVCAM/DV mode, audio, mic noise reduction)

SETUP MENU (clock, display character size)

ETC (OTHER) (beep, display, record indicator, color bars, hours meter)

Set Timecode Hour

1. Press the **SEL/PUSH EXEC** jog dial to see our choices of Timecode Settings.

We'll see that a third column appears with choices that branch out from the middle column.

Let's work on the first choice of timecode settings: TC PRESET.

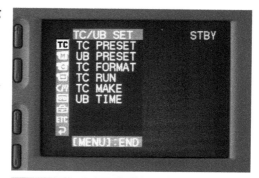

2. We see that timecode defaults to 00:00:00:00.

But, we want to begin at hour 01.

We usually want to begin each tape at a different hour or half-hour to avoid duplicate times in editing.

Since TC PRESET is highlighted, we press the jog dial.

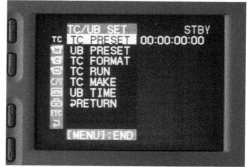

3. We are now are presented with 3 choices: RESET, PRESET or RETURN.

Turn the jog dial until PRESET is highlighted, and then press in to select it.

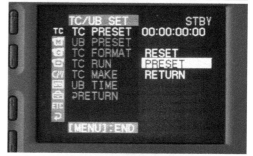

4. The hours are highlighted. Turn the jog dial to get to 01. Press it. Since we want minutes, seconds and frames to be 00, we have to press the jog dial three more times until the cursor highlights SET. Press the jog dial.

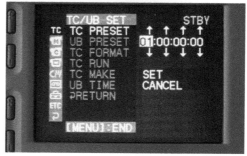

5. We're now back to the main TC/UB Menu. If we want to reset timecode, we can go back into the TC PRESET Menu, and highlight RESET to get back to 00:00:00:00

To accept a setting quickly, we can press the **MENU** button to accept our last choice. Or, we can scroll down to RETURN on the menu and select it.

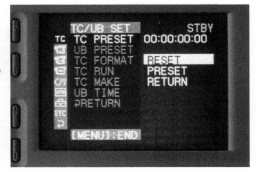

Set Non Drop Frame Timecode

1. Jog down to TC FORMAT.

The camera's default is AUTO, but I think your editor would be happier if it said NDF (Non Drop Frame).

If NDF doesn't appear in the right-hand column, push the **SEL/PUSH EXEC** jog dial.

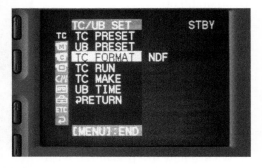

2. The choice is AUTO, DF or NDF. Unless you are using Drop Frame timecode (which is usually used for direct broadcast, but is less useful for general editing), I suggest NDF (Non Drop-Frame). Rotate the jog dial until NDF is highlighted in yellow, and press the dial to choose it.

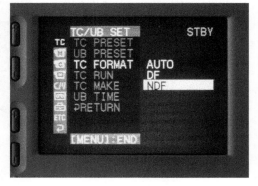

Set User Bits

User Bits contain additional information that can be helpful in editing. If you're shooting a large project over many days, it is conceivable there will be several tapes with the same hours-minutes-seconds timecode.

To prevent duplication, it's helpful to use the User Bits to enter the date and camera identification. Jog down to UB PRESET, and push.

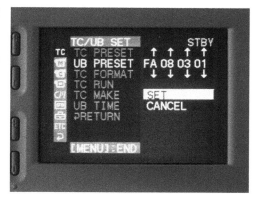

The cursor hovers over one of four groups of letter/number combinations. Use the jog wheel to change the numbers, and push to accept it and move to the next group. Push SET when you're happy.

Letters only go up to "FF," so if your last name is Godard, Hathaway, or Zemeckis, you'll have to think up some other initials.

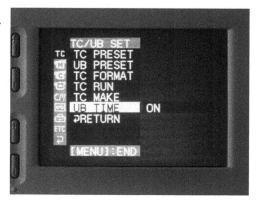

User Bit Time

Alternatively, you can let the User Bits show the actual time of day instead of manually setting the date once a day.

Remember, User Bits are not "burned in" over the picture, which is a good thing. They only appear when deciphered by the timecode reader in your playback deck.

Set UB TIME: ON to enable the actual time of day to be recorded as User Bits. Turn UB TIME: OFF if you want your own User Bits recorded.

TC RUN: REC RUN

Sets Timecode Run to Record Run, which means that our tape will have continuous timecode, without breaks or interruptions. If we make the other choice, FREE RUN, timecode will be recorded according to the actual time of day, and there will be breaks in the timecode whenever we stop the camera. There are advantages to both.

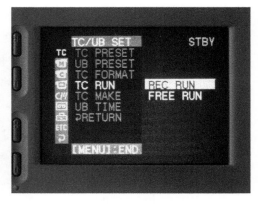

Most editors prefer REC RUN, because they can digitize (load) the tape without having to worry about breaks in the timecode. Usually, the nonlinear editing software will detect a timecode break, and treat each break as a separate shot—which may not be the editor's intention.

With FREE RUN, every start-stop of the camera will cause a break in the timecode, and we'll wind up with lots of shorter digitized clips in our editing bin.

TC MAKE: REGEN

Timecode is either Regenerated or Preset. TIMECODE: REGEN prevents timecode breaks even if the tape is reviewed or ejected. Free Run timecode should use the Preset setting.

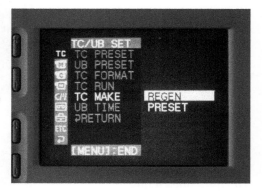

Timecode Summary of Recommended Settings

TC PRESET   PRESET to different hour for each tape

UB PRESET   PRESET to camera ID and date

TC FORMAT   NDF (Non Drop Frame)

TC RUN   REC RUN (Record Run)

TC MAKE   REGEN (Regenerate Timecode)

UB TIME   OFF (if you are going to enter camera ID and date
         ON to have the camera enter actual time of day

More Menu Settings

Now that we know how to navigate the menu, I'll just explain my recommended settings below. Illustrations appear only occasionally.

M - MANUAL SET

AUTO SHUTTER: ON
(helps to compensate for exposure in extremely bright or dark conditions)

PROG. SCAN: OFF
(which means that Interlaced Scanning is on. Progressive scan is useful for stills, but when recording video, it is not a true 30 frame per second rate, which results in some field doubling and possibly jittery action.)

SETUP: 0%
(7.0% reduces contrast by making shadows and black areas a little "milkier.")

C - CAMERA SET

D ZOOM: OFF
(Turn OFF Digital Zoom, which can introduce artifacts to the image. Use optical zoom only.)

16:9WIDE: OFF
(Turning 16:9 aspect ratio off allows us to record in 4:3 Standard TV format, using all the CCD pixels.) This double-negative menu setting is sort of like saying "Yes, we have no bananas today." Think of this important choice as meaning 4:3 Standard ON.

If you're shooting for theatrical release or widescreen TV, you might consider 16:9. But remember, you're using fewer horizontal lines of resolution, and fewer pixels. I'd consider an optical anamorphic lens adapter.

STEADYSHOT: ON
(activates optical image stabilization. Does not degrade picture.)

FRAME REC: OFF
(if this is on, you'll be shooting stop-motion animation.)

INT. REC: OFF
(if this is on, you're doing timelapse.)

WIND: OFF
(if this is on, a noise-cancelling circuit reduces wind noise.)

LCD/VF SET

LCD B.L: NORMAL (uses less battery power to Back Light the LCD viewing screen. BRIGHT makes it easier to see the LCD viewing screen in bright exteriors like snow. When the AC adapter/charger is plugged in, this menu item, along with VF B.L. can't be changed because they automatically jump to BRIGHT.

LCD COLOR should be in the middle, normal position

VF B.L: NORMAL (to conserve battery power)

GUIDEFRAME:OFF

(Guideframe ON will superimpose a rectangle over the center 1/8th of the screen. Its size has no significance other than to help level the horizon or see the center of the image. Pretend it's a viewfinder crosshair, only more distracting under normal shooting conditions.

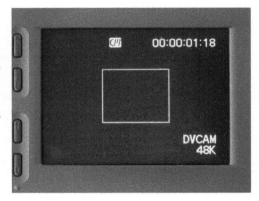

TAPE SET

REC MODE: DVCAM
(This is important. You don't want to be surprised to learn that you've just spent the entire day shooting DV format on DVCAM tape.)

AUDIO MODE: FS48K
(48K, 16-bit audio is higher quality than the other choice, 32K, 12-bit)

MIC NR: ON (microphone noise reduction on.)

AUDIO SET: AGC CH1: ON (for Automatic Gain Control On.)
            AGC CH2: ON

However, here's a helpful alternative:

AUDIO SET: AGC CH1: ON (Automatic Gain Control On.)
            AGC CH2: OFF (Manual Gain enabled on channel 2.)

Here's how it works: the single shotgun mic is plugged into INPUT 1, and split into two tracks. Channel 1 has automatic gain (level) control. Channel 2 has manual level control. So, when you push the AUDIO LEVEL button on the back of the camera, you're only adjusting Channel 2. I usually leave Channel 2 about 20dB less than Channel 1 to compensate for loud noises.

ETC - OTHERS

DATE REC: OFF

Very important!

This is one of the most important menu choices of all. Forgetting this setting means the date and time will be permanently superimposed over every scene forever. You probably don't want this. To be sure the date and time are not recorded, make sure you select "OFF," and double-check that you do not see the date and

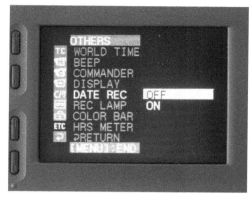

time in the viewfinder or on the LCD viewing screen when recording.

[MENU]: END

Pushing the MENU button now, or at any time, will save the settings entered so far, and will exit the menu.

Final Check

After setting up your menu, there's one last thing to verify. Keep the LCD Viewing Screen open. Turn the Main Power Switch **OFF**. Then turn it on again to **CAMERA**.

The LCD Viewing screen should display the following:

1. DATE and TIME should be visible at the bottom of the screen for about two seconds, and then disappear.

2. At the middle right side of the screen, you should see DVCAM (to indicate format) and 48K (audio mode).

3. The top right of the screen should show CM if your cassette has a built-in memory chip, STBY for Standby Mode (waiting to record), and the timecode.

4. Push the **TC/U-Bit** button to toggle between timecode and user bits.

5. Push the DISPLAY button to see a clear, text-free screen. All text and numbers should disappear, except the green STBY letters. If you see the date and time at the bottom of the screen, they will be recorded on tape. You probably don't want this.

Ready to Roll

Get ready to roll with the Main Power Switch in the **CAMERA** position. This is called the Standby position, because the camera is standing by for you to push the red Record button.

On the DSR-PD150, you have a choice of two buttons to push to record. The main one is at the back.

The other Record button is located on top.

Pause recording by pressing either button again.

Turn the Main Power Switch **OFF** in between setups if you want to conserve battery power.

Manual Functions

In addition to the automatic functions, the DSR-PD150 offers manual control of:

- Zoom
- Focus
- Iris
- Shutter speed
- Gain
- AE (Auto Exposure) Shift
- White Balance
- Custom Preset (Color Level, Sharpness, White Balance Shift, AGC)
- ND Filters 1 and 2 (1/4 and 1/32)
- Spotlight Button (for example, someone on stage under a spotlight)
- Backlight Button
- Audio Recording Level: Separate or Linked, CH1 and CH2
- Zebra Stripes (100% or 70%)

Viewfinder

The viewfinder is black and white.

Below the eyepiece, you'll find a small lever to adjust the eyepiece diopter to your vision. Aim at a distant object, and move the lever until the image in the eyepiece is sharpest.

Use the standard eyecup if you wear glasses.

The camera comes with an additional, larger, rubber eyecup that some camera operators find helpful in bright sunlight because it wraps around ones face. This eyecup will accept soft chamois eye cushions, available at many camera rental companies, to coddle delicate cheeks.

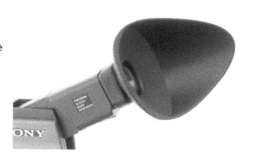

Cleaning viewfinder.

To separate the viewfinder for cleaning, there may be a piece of tape covering the release lever. Peel off the tape, push the RELEASE lever down, and slide the upper finder assembly in the direction of the arrow (up). To remove dust, gently blow with Dust-Off. Smudges may be removed with a micro-fibre cloth. Do NOT use lens fluid or solvents. Some of the elements are plastic and may be damaged

Custom Preset

Pushing the **CUSTOM PRESET** button, located on top of the camera behind the handgrip, brings up a menu of settings that can be customized and saved for the duration of a production (or longer).

To invoke Custom Preset, CP SET: ON must be selected.

The LCD screen or viewfinder will display your other current choices, which can be changed. These include:

Color Level (saturation), Image Sharpness, White Balance shift, and Auto Gain Control Limit.

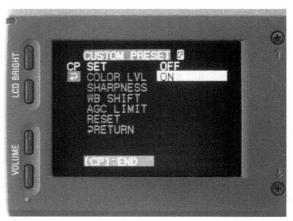

Of these, AGC LIMIT is probably the most useful. Limiting the camcorder's Auto Gain circuitry to 6 or 12 dB will prevent the noise or "graininess" that can occur when shooting in low light with gain cranked all the way up.

The rest of the settings are a matter of personal taste. I like the default settings, which can always be restored by going to RESET.

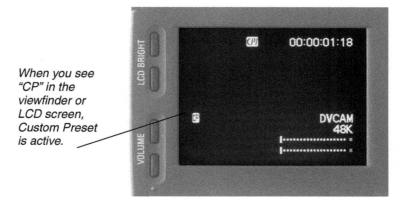

When you see "CP" in the viewfinder or LCD screen, Custom Preset is active.

DSR-250

The DSR-250 is the least expensive shoulder-resting camcorder that accepts both Mini and Standard (the larger size) DVCAM or DV cassettes. At a little more than the price of a DSR-PD150, and about two pounds heavier, you can have the comfort of a camera that snuggles on your shoulder all day for well-balanced handheld shooting, with tapes that last three hours without having to reload. This makes it a perfect camera for wedding videographers, event, educational and corporate users. It's a good camera for schools to record graduations, school plays and sports events.

When I first saw the DSR-250, I was alarmed that the camcorder did not have an interchangeable lens. How could it be a serious, professional contender? I had been brought up in an industry that demanded a wide array of lenses and choices. After using the camera, however, I have changed my mind. There are benefits as well.

Olympus adopted a similar approach with its wildly popular E-10 digital still camera, with its fixed zoom lens, which shot most of the photos in this book. The design philosophy behind the attached zoom is that dust and dirt cannot fly onto the CCD or prism when you change lenses. You don't have to worry about adjusting back-focus, because the lens is permanently and rigidly mounted. Furthermore, the overall size can be reduced by integrating some of the lens' electronics into the camera body, providing image stabilization, electric zoom, along with automatic or manual focus, zoom and iris.

DSR-250

DSR-PD150

The DSR-250 uses the same lens, 1/3" CCDs, and LCD viewing screen as the DSR-PD150.

The DSR-250's larger body accommodates a 3-hour "Standard" cassette, uses professional style 12-volt batteries, and quickly goes from hand-held shoulder-resting mode to tripod.

Like the DSR-PD150, the DSR-250 has a built-in 2.5" color 200K dot (880 x 228 pixels) LCD that flips out from the rear operator's side. This is a welcome addition rarely found on professional camcorders. The 1.5" black and white viewfinder has 600 lines of horizontal resolution, so images snap into crisp focus when focusing manually. Unlike the DSR-PD150, the 250 viewfinder and the monitor can operate at the same time, which can be helpful, for example, alternately checking focus in the viewfinder and then following fast-moving action with the monitor from a tripod.

Like the DSR-PD150, there are three 1/3" CCDs with 380,000 pixels providing interlace scan for moving video, and progressive scan for stills. The lens is a fixed 12x zoom, with Super Steady Shot to optically stabilize the image. The DSR-250 captures still images as JPEG files on a Memory Stick at 640 x 480 resolution.

SMPTE timecode controls are similar to the DSR-PD150.

So, why should we use a DSR-250? Although we see lots of DSR-PD150 camcorders on local news crews, I'm afraid there's a prejudice of camcorder size that might prevail if we arrived at the Democratic National Convention with one. I suspect the DSR-250 could easily pass muster and not raise any suspicious eyebrows. Of course, if you had a DSR-500WS...

Thus, advantage number one: the DSR-250 looks serious. It's the kind of camera we didn't want to have when we bought a DSR-PD100A or DSR-PD150, when we wanted to be inconspicuous and look like a tourist. The DSR-250 is not going to be confused with an amateur camcorder.

A brief digression—a production tale:

Once upon a time (not too long ago), just out of college, I bought a Beaulieu R-16 16mm camera for expedition and ski jobs. It was lightweight, tiny, easily fit into a backpack, had a clever battery that doubled as a handgrip, ran slow motion and did everything an adventure cameraman could want. This was just before video supplanted film at the networks.

I think camera design is often influenced by country of origin. The rival Swiss Bolex looks like a cuckoo clock—boxy, functional, spring-wound. The French Beaulieu was used extensively by news crews covering their country's tenure in Vietnam, but it still looked like an ornate cooking utensil. It even has historical allusions: a guillotine shutter, with a mirrored surface, sliced back and forth in front of the film plane to alternately expose the image or bounce it into the viewfinder.
The Beaulieu and I went all over the world together, shooting freelance assignments for *National Geographic* and ABC. We filmed whitewater

kayaking and skiing in the Alps, hang gliding in the Rockies, avalanches in Switzerland, glaciers in Alaska. But these were solitary adventures, in that the crew never exceeded a couple of assistants or sherpas and, of course, the objects and subjects of our attention.

But these were not, I was assured, the cinematographic big leagues. So, one day, I managed to get the attention of John Wilcox and Toni Brown at ABC Sports. I was hired to film the World Kayak Championships in Muotathal, Switzerland as the whitewater and rig specialist. Looking back now, I fear I might have been the expendable cameraman—the one who does the point-of-view shots and the agony-of-defeat angles.

Cut to the Swiss Alps. It's my first morning on a real film crew. The other cameramen, all famous names, looked at me (and my little Beaulieu) the way someone might look at a tray that has just been dropped in a fine restaurant: a mixture of dismay and disdain and horror. They all had their venerable Arriflex 16BL and 16S cameras, Frezzis and CP-16s. Any one of these cameras could have been used to hammer nails, I thought. But they did indeed look much more serious and professional than the toy-like French confection I was using. Never mind that they all took the same pictures, used the same lenses, and were equally steady. Never mind that I could rig my camera to the front of a kayak in a splash bag, while a Frezzi would probably sink it, or that I could throw my Beaulieu into a pack, along with lenses, magazines and film, and climb the adjacent mountain to get a high-angle establishing shot. The Beaulieu just wasn't considered professional. It was just too small and too light.

So, now that we've established that the DSR-250 won't look puny, what other compelling features does it have over the DSR-PD150 that will induce us to spend a few dollars more?

The main difference is ergonomics when hand-held, or more accurately, shoulder-resting. The 250 has a soft, form-fitting pad on its base that conforms to your shoulder. The viewfinder adjusts front-back, up-down and left-right to wherever your eyepoint happens to be. Most controls are easier to access than the DSR-PD150, with lots of analog switches, instead of menu choices, to turn things on and off.

The DSR-250 uses Sony BP-L40A, BP-L60A, and BP-L90A Lithium-Ion batteries that mount directly to the back of the camcorder. These are the same 12-volt batteries that are used on many other professional cameras, including the Sony DSR-300A and DSR-500WS DVCAM Camcorders. A single BP-L90A will power the camcorder for about nine hours. Anton Bauer batteries can be attached with the optional QR-DSR Gold Mount.

DSR-PD250 Camera Views

Front

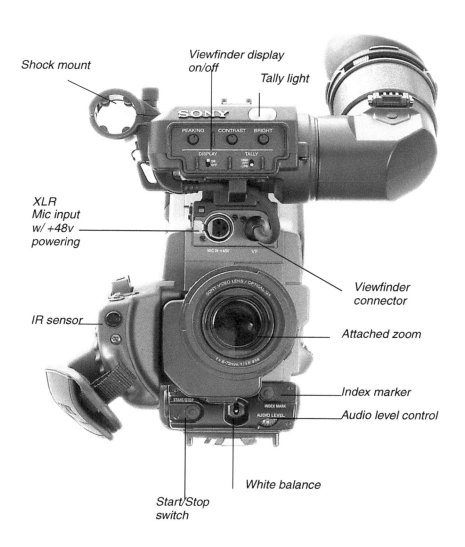

Shock mount

Viewfinder display on/off

Tally light

XLR Mic input w/ +48v powering

Viewfinder connector

IR sensor

Attached zoom

Index marker

Audio level control

White balance

Start/Stop switch

Rear

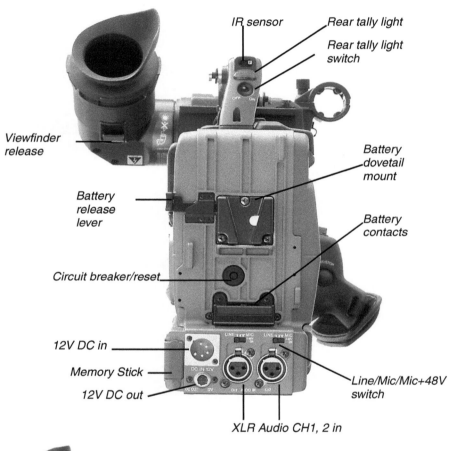

IR sensor

Rear tally light

Rear tally light switch

Viewfinder release

Battery dovetail mount

Battery release lever

Battery contacts

Circuit breaker/reset

12V DC in

Memory Stick

12V DC out

Line/Mic/Mic+48V switch

XLR Audio CH1, 2 in

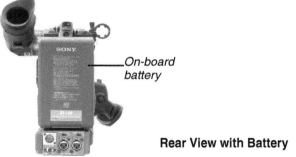

On-board battery

Rear View with Battery

Top

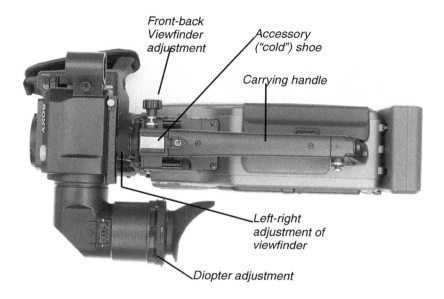

Front-back
Viewfinder
adjustment

Accessory
("cold") shoe

Carrying handle

Left-right
adjustment of
viewfinder

Diopter adjustment

Bottom

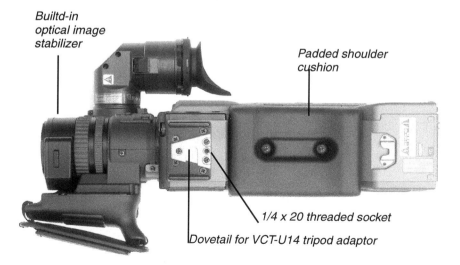

Builtd-in
optical image
stabilizer

Padded shoulder
cushion

1/4 x 20 threaded socket

Dovetail for VCT-U14 tripod adaptor

Camera Left

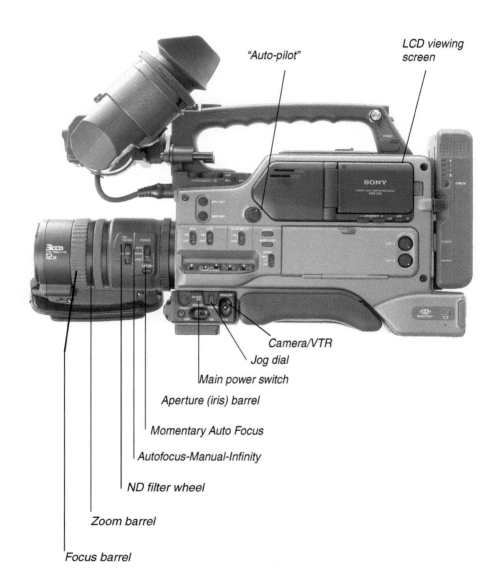

"Auto-pilot"

LCD viewing
screen

Camera/VTR

Jog dial

Main power switch

Aperture (iris) barrel

Momentary Auto Focus

Autofocus-Manual-Infinity

ND filter wheel

Zoom barrel

Focus barrel

Camera Right

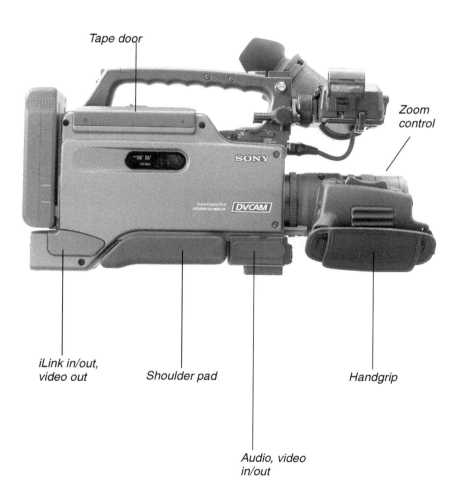

Tape door

Zoom
control

iLink in/out,
video out

Shoulder pad

Handgrip

Audio, video
in/out

DSR-250 Jump Start

Attach the Battery

When you buy a DSR-250, be aware that it doesn't come with a battery or charger in the box. Its 12-14 volt battery pack is the familiar one common to most professional video camcorders, and attaches onto a dovetail at the rear.

1. Line up the index mark on the battery with the line on the camera.

2.Slide down until you hear it snap in place. The index mark on the camera should align with the word **LOCK** on the battery.

The 4-pin male XLR receptacle at the rear of the DSR-250 accepts power cables from an external 12-14 volt battery or an AC to DC power supply, such as Sony's AC-550.

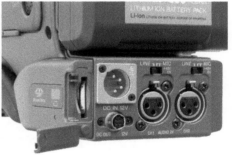

You can find adapters for Makita and DeWalt cordless drill batteries, as well as fused cables for your car battery. Use them wisely—they make service managers cringe at the thought of mishap and meltdown.

To remove the battery, press the battery release button on the camcorder. Lift up on the battery, and then pull it away from the camera.

The contact points at the bottom of the battery should be cleaned occasionally with contact cleaner and a foam swab.

Attach the Microphone

You'll recognize the ECN-NV1
microphone of the DSR-250 from
the DSR-PD150.

Plug the 3-pin XLR microphone
connector into **MIC IN +48v**
phantom powered XLR receptacle
on the front of the camera.

When the wind is howling, use a
foam windscreen, and slide the
MIC LOW CUT switch to the **ON**
position to reduce rumble.

(The receptacle to the right
provides power to an accessory
on-board video light or obie light).

Power up the Camcorder

Turn the main **POWER** switch
ON.

Set the **MEMORY-CAMERA-VTR**
selector switch to **CAMERA**.

The **MEMORY** position is for
taking "stills" on a Memory
Stick.

The **VTR** position is, of course,
for playback.

Note the convenient location
of the **SEL/PUSH EXEC** jog
dial. More on this later.

Set the Microphone Controls

Fully Automatic

Open the control panel door below the LCD Viewing Screen.

To record audio from the on-board microphone onto two tracks, slide both **AUDIO INPUT** switches to **FRONT** (meaning that the front XLR receptacle is active for both Channel 1 and Channel 2 audio.)

Slide both **AUDIO SELECT** switches to **AUTO** for fully automatic gain control.

CH-1 Manual - CH-2 Auto

However, why not split the audio from the on-board mic, which is mono anyway, onto two separate tracks—one manually controlled, and the other automatic. That way, you'll have an automatic backup in case you're late responding to a level change, and you'll be able to manually ride the gain.

Be sure to indicate how the tracks are split on the tape cassette case or production notes, so your editor will know what you've done.

Set **CH-1** to **MANUAL** and slide **CH-2** to **AUTO**.

If you're shooting from a tripod and using the LCD viewing screen, you'll probably find it easiest to adjust audio levels by turning the **CH-1 AUDIO LEVEL** knob. (You can see it even when the control panel door is closed, but it's easier to grab with the door open).

Push the **AUDIO LEVEL** button to display the VU meter in the viewfinder or LCD screen.

If you're shooting handheld, it's much easier to control the audio level of channel 1 with your left thumb on the **AUDIO LEVEL** control at the front of the camera, under the lens.

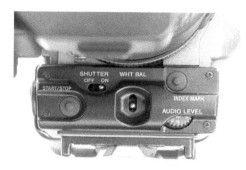

The front **AUDIO LEVEL** knob only controls audio coming from the front XLR microphone receptacle going to Channel 1. It's wired in series with the **CH-1 AUDIO LEVEL** knob at the rear. So, when you use the front level control, turn the rear one almost fully clockwise (loudest) for the most range.

Audio Monitor Speaker

A built-in speaker facilitates audio monitoring while handheld.

If you're splitting tracks and recording channel 1 manually, it's a good idea to slide the **AUDIO MONITOR** switch to **CH-1**.

Adjust the volume of the built-in speaker with the **MONITOR** dial.

Headphones

Plug headphones into the mini receptacle at the rear of the handle.

Moulded single-ear "buds" like the ones for cell-phones are comfortable and help reduce ambient noise.

Rear of Handle

The funny little screw above the headphone receptacle is for a carrying strap.

The **OFF - ON** switch at the rear of the handle turns the rear tally light off, in case you don't want people behind you to know when you are recording.

Load Tape

Tape can be loaded with the camcorder's Main Power Switch in any position.

Open the tape compartment lid, and insert either a Mini or Standard size DVCAM tape.

You can also use Mini or Standard DV tape.

Press the blue **EJECT** button to remove the cassette.

 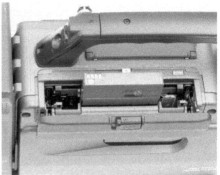

Adjust Viewfinder

The viewfinder diopter setting adjusts the image to your eye focus, so you don't have to wear glasses while shooting. If your glasses are greater than -3 or +0, accessory diopters can be ordered.

The recommended way to adjust eyepiece focus is to zoom out wide and adjust the diopter until the image is sharpest.

Next, find the most comfortable position for the camera to rest on your shoulder. Adjust the viewfinder position relative to your eye with by loosening the front-back and left-right knobs.

Electronic Controls for Viewfinder

There are a few more controls to fiddle with at the front of the viewfinder. The default positions for BRIGHT (brightness), CONTRAST and PEAKING are with the index marks pointing to 12 o'clock. These controls only adjust the black and white viewfinder image—they will not do anything to the image being recorded.

Peaking adjusts the perceived sharpness of edges—increasing it can sometimes aid focus in low light, as can boosting brightness and contrast.

DISPLAY turns the on-screen information **ON** and **OFF**: battery status, timecode, tape remaining, tape format, audio format and manual audio levels. This switch is wired in series with the secondary **DISPLAY** button on the camera right side—so it's a good idea to leave it on.

If you don't want the blinking red light at the front of the camera to advertise when you're rolling, or if you don't want it relecting in the eyeglasses of the person being interviewed right in front of you, turn the front **TALLY** switch **OFF**. You can also adjust its brightness to make it more visible in bright sunlight or less distracting in dimly lit areas.

Beneath the TALLY switch, on the viewfinder under-belly, there's a three-way slide switch that turns on a white LED lens light to help you see some of the front controls at night.

DSR-250 Auto-Pilot Settings

If, at this point you can't wait any longer and must shoot something immediately, here's a checklist of the switches to set for cruise-control:

1. **ND FILTER: OFF**

2. **FOCUS: AUTO**

3. **AUTO MODE: ON** (over-rides individual settings of ATW, AGC, IRIS, and SHUTTER)

You're ready to roll. There are two **START/STOP** switches: one beneath your thumb at the rear of the handgrip, and the other at the front of the camera body, on the right side, below the lens.

DSR-250 Manual Settings

The DSR-250 provides a great degree of manual control over most settings, for consistent exposure, color and quality.

AUTO MODE: OFF

Disable automatic control of exposure and color (white balance, gain, shutter and aperture) by switching **AUTO MODE OFF**.

You can then decide whether to have white balance, gain, shutter and aperture manually or automatically adjusted. If you're a Type-A person like me, you'll want to retain as much manual control as possible, and you'll set the **AGC** and **ATW** switches to the **OFF** positions, the **SHUTTER** switch to **ON**, and the **IRIS** to **MANUAL**.

AGC: OFF

If we leave Automatic Gain Control on, the camera's electronics may help us out in low-light situations by boosting the signal to make it appear brighter. While this is often useful, it can introduce noise or artifacts to the signal, which can look "grainy." Furthermore, if we're setting the aperture manually to make a scene look deliberately dark (a day-for-night scene, for example) Automatic Gain Control will negate our efforts by trying to compensate.

Turning the **AGC** switch **OFF** turns off *automatic* gain control, and, at the same time, enables the 3-position **GAIN** switch below it. When gain is more than 3 dB, the amber GAIN UP indicator glows in the viewfinder. The factory settings are:

L (low)   0 dB boost in gain
M (medium)   9 dB
H (high)   18 dB

Each of the 3 **GAIN** settings can be re-programmed from the Menu in 3 dB steps from 0 to 18 dB, so you might want to change **M** to 6 dB and **H** to 9 dB. The amount of gain chosen is displayed in the eyepiece or LCD screen.

To change the menu settings, push the MENU switch in the direction of its arrow, turn the SEL/PUSH EXEC jog wheel to MANUAL SET, select GAIN LEVEL, and then make your choices for **H**, **M** and **L**.

ATW: OFF

The simplest way to control color balance on the DSR-250 is to pretend you're using color still or motion picture film, which comes in two flavors: balanced for daylight (5600°K) or balanced for tungsten lights (3200°K).

The two presets on the DSR-250 offer similar choices, 3200° K or 5800° K — and you engage them as follows:

1. Set **ATW OFF**.

2. Set **WHITE BAL** to **PRESET**. Actually, this switch could be relabeled "Color Temperature," to distinguish it from the White Balance switch at the front of the camera.

3. Set the adjacent switch to either **3200° K** or **5800° K**.

The viewfinder or viewing screen will show an icon of the sun for 5800°K, or a light bulb for 3200°K. In reality, very few light bulbs, with the exception of 211, 212, and other specialty bulbs, are exactly that color temperature. Most household bulbs measure around 2800°K, and will render a warm, amber-like tone—which is not necessarily a bad thing. Similarly, outdoor light at sunset is very close to 3200°K. Yet the golden tones at sunset and magic hour are often beautiful, but would be "corrected" back to neutral if we shot it with the white balance set to automatic.

The other way to ruin sunsets or beautiful interior lighting is to overuse the A and B manual presets. Manual presets are a wonderful way to remove the green component of fluorescents and mercury vapor lamps. They are also the best way to correct for errant HMI lights or off-color production lamps when you really do want the subject or product to be shot under neutral illumination. Perhaps we're doing a product shot of a strand of lustrous white pearls adorning a beautiful, ivory-skinned model. The client will not be happy if the white pearls suddenly mutated into a greenish South Sea variety, no matter how rare, nor will the model's entourage of makeup artists, stylists and agents be satisfied if she is suddenly given a complexion not recognized in her lengthy contract.

Here's how to manually lock in pure whites under the current illumination:

Slide the 3-position **WHITE BAL** switch to **A** or **B**.

Fill the frame by zooming in on a white showcard or other pure white object in the frame.

Momentarily pull the **WHT BAL** switch up—it's located under the lens at the front of the camera.

The white balance icon flashes for a few seconds in the eyepiece, and remains steady once it has acquired its information, along with A or B, depending on which of the two white balance memory locations it has been stored. The white balance "memories" are useful when moving back and forth between two locations or setups. Slide the **WHITE BAL** switch to **A** or **B**.

 A

 B

SHUTTER: ON

If left unattended, on automatic, the internal electronic shutter of the camcorder could expose each frame as quickly as 1/10,000 second to compensate for extremely bright lighting conditions. Although high shutter speeds are good for reducing motion blur of tennis backhands or droplets of liquids, they can also appear jittery or strobing when played back.

To keep the shutter at its default 1/60th second exposure, providing what is arguably the most acceptable speed for most people's persistence of vision, slide the **SHUTTER** switch **OFF**. You should see the speed displayed as the denominator (60) in the viewfinder.

To control the shutter manually, you have to turn the **SHUTTER** switch **ON**. This is somewhat counter-intuitive, since we just learned to turn **AGC** and **ATW OFF** for manual control. In my camera retrofit kit, which includes suggestions of every camera I've ever used, I'd include three small labels with "**MANUAL**" printed in small letters on a P-Touch, to cover the contradictory ON and OFF epithets.

Once the SHUTTER switch is ON (MANUAL), the shutter speed itself is changed from the Menu. Engage the MENU switch to bring the menu up in the viewfinder or viewing screen. Turn the jog dial to MANUAL SET. Select SHUTTER SPEED. The jog dial will offer choices from 1/4 second to 1/10,000 second. A "NO SHUTTER" menu selection will result in a 1/60th second shutter setting, and prevents AUTO SHUTTER from turning on

Your choice will be displayed in the viewfinder once the Menu is cleared.

IRIS: MAN

The aperture (iris) of the lens can be set manually by sliding the **IRIS** switch to Manual, as long as the **AUTO MODE** is **OFF**.

In this position, a quick squeeze with your right pinkie on the **PUSH AUTO** microswitch restores the picture to an automatically calculated F stop.

The F Stop of the lens is displayed in the viewfinder, from F1.6 (wide open) to F11 (stopped down) and on to CLOSE, which is totally dark.

Once the iris is in manual mode, the actual adjustment is made by rotating the aperture ring on the lens. Turn the barrel *Clockwise to Close* the lens (from your point-of-view operating the camera).

While we're on the lens, the focus ring is turned *Clockwise for Closer* objects.

The zoom ring is turned *Clockwise to go Wider*.

Lens

When the lens is set to **MANUAL FOCUS**, the icon of a hand appears in the viewfinder. Momentarily sliding the switch to INFINITY does just that, and quickly pressing **PUSH AUTO** is a good way to find focus at opportune times (not during a critical, historical or un-repeatable moment).

If you see the letters ND1 or ND2 flashing in the finder (only when the Iris is on Auto), the camcorder is telling you to engage one of two neutral density (gray optical glass) filters. When the filter has been selected, the letters will stop flashing. ND OFF means you're cutting down too much light, and you should disengage the ND filters.

Be sure the ND filter setting lines up with the index mark. Halfway positions will degrade the image because you're shooting part of the filter holder.

Zebra, Zoom, etc

Using the zebra stripes, zoom, exposure, Memory Stick and other features of the camcorder are covered later on, in "Common Features: All Models" beginning page 129.

Menu Selections

Most of the Menu settings of the DSR-250 are similar to the DSR-PD150. See the DSR-PD150 chapter for a more detailed overview.

Push the **MENU** switch down to bring it up on screen. Push the **MENU** switch down again to save your selections and hide the text.

Rotate the **SEL/PUSH EXEC** jog dial to *change* selections. Push in on the jog dial to *make* a selection.

Like the DSR-PD150, the Main Menu is organized as follows:

Timecode (timecode, user bits, timecode format, etc.)

Manual Settings (shutter, scan mode, black level)

Camera Settings (digital zoom, 16:9/4:3, SteadyShot, timelapse, etc.)

LCD/VF Settings (LCD screen and viewfinder options)

CM Settings (cassette memory functions like title, erase, etc)

TAPE Settings (DVCAM/DV mode, audio mode, tape remaining, audio reference level)

SETUP MENU (clock, display character size, Li-Ion or NiCad Battery)

ETC (OTHER) (beep, display, record indicator, color bars, odometer)

To save a setting quickly, we can press the **MENU** button to accept our last choice. Or, we can scroll down to RETURN on the menu and select it.

Some Menu selections follow, with recommendations starred.

TC/UB SET

TC Preset

RESET to return to 00:00:00:00
*PRESET to enter your own timecode start time.

UB Preset
RESET to return User Bits to 00:00:00:00
*PRESET to enter your own information: date and camera identification,
from 00 to FF.

TC FORMAT
AUTO (default setting, but you should change this)
DF Drop Frame
*NDF Non Drop Frame

TC RUN
*REC RUN (continuous timecode, without breaks or interruptions)
FREE RUN, (actual time of day, with breaks in the timecode)

TC MAKE
*REGEN
FREE RUN

UB TIME
*OFF (to enable recording of your own preset User Bits, described above)
ON (actual time of day recorded as User Bits).
to have the camera enter actual time of day

MANUAL SET

SHUTTER SPEED
*60 (1/60th second)
4 - 10,000 (1/4 - 1/10,000 second

GAIN LEVEL
H *9   (0-18 dB)
M *6   (0-18 dB)
L *0   (0-18 dB)

AUTO SHUTTER
ON (default)
*OFF

PROG. SCAN
*OFF   (interlaced)
ON   (useful for stills. actually
records at 15 frames per second
motion)

SETUP
*0%
7% (higher black level)

CAMERA SET

D ZOOM
*OFF
24x (12x is optical, and remaining 12x is digital)
48x (12x optical, 36x digital)

16:9WIDE
*OFF (records in standard TV 4:3 aspect ratio, which is same as 1.33:1)
ON (16:9 aspect ratio—by using center area of CCD only)

STEADYSHOT
*ON (optical image stabilization)
OFF

FRAME REC
*OFF
ON (stop-motion, almost single frame, "burst" animation.)

INT. REC
*OFF
ON   (interval recording—more surveillance style than timelapse)
SET   set INTERVAL between exposures (30 seconds to 10 minutes)
        and RECORD TIME of each burst (.5 to 2 seconds)

LCD SET

LCD COLOR
*middle is default—right is warmer, left is cooler)

GUIDEFRAME
*OFF
ON   (superimposed rectangle in center 1/8th of the screen).

CM SET

TAPE TITLE
Tapes with Cassette Memory chips can be labeled. When the cassette is loaded into camcorder or VTR, the title will be displayed for 5 seconds

ITEM ERASE
Deletes selective items stored on the Cassette Memory chip

ERASE ALL
Deletes all data stored in the Cassette Memory chip

TAPE SET

REC MODE
*DVCAM (Important. You don't want to be surprised to learn that you've
	just spent the entire day shooting DV format on DVCAM tape.)
DV SP (Standard Play)

AUDIO MODE
FS32K	(12 bit, 4 channels)
*FS48K	(16 bit, 2 channels)

TAPE REMAIN
AUTO	(displays tape remaining for 8 seconds when camera is first
	turned on and for 8 seconds when you push **DISPLAY**.)
ON	(continuous display of tape remaining)

A REF LVL (AUDIO REFERENCE LEVEL)
-12dB	(standard DV level)
* -20 dB	(more headroom for safety, less chance of distortion from over-
	modulation, preferred level by many editors.)

SETUP MENU

CLOCK	(set date and time)
LTR SIZE	(*NORMAL or 2x)

BATTERY REMAIN
*LI-ION	(use this setting to calculate remaining power with Li-Ion
	Sony batteries
Ni-CD	(use this for NiCad Sony batteries)

ETC - OTHERS

WORLD TIME
*0
Set deviation from standard time entered, such as daylight savings, etc.

BEEP
MELODY
*NORMAL
OFF

COMMANDER
*ON (Receiving Remote Control signals is enabled)
OFF

DISPLAY

LCD   (picture displayed in viewfinder and LCD viewing screen)
V-OUT/LCD   (picture displayed on a monitor as well, from Video Out)

EXT RECCTL

OFF
ON   (**START/STOP** button of camcorder enables simultaneous record
      and pause of a VTR connected to camcorder via i.Link cable)

DATE REC

***OFF (Very important! This is one of the most important menu choices
      of all. Forgetting this setting means the date and time will be
      superimposed over every scene forever. You probably don't want
      this. To be sure the date and time are not recorded, make sure you
      select "OFF," and double-check that you do not see the date and
      time in the viewfinder or on the LCD viewing screen when
      recording.)

ON   (Are you sure? You're probably doing legal work or something that
      needs the date and time superimposed over every shot.)

COLOR BAR

ON displays standard full field color bars

HRS METER

Shows how much time the camcorder has been on.

Final Check

After setting up your menu, there's one last thing to verify. Turn the Main
Power Switch **OFF**, then **ON**. Slide the **VTR-CAMERA** switch to **CAMERA**.

The Viewfinder or LCD Viewing screen should display the following:

1. DATE and TIME should be visible at the bottom of the screen for about
two seconds, and then disappear.

2. At the middle right side of the screen, you should see DVCAM (to
indicate format) and 48K (audio mode) for best quality audio.

3. The top right of the screen should show CM if your cassette has a built-
in memory chip, STBY for Standby Mode (waiting to record), and the
timecode.

4. Push the **DISPLAY** button to clear distracting text. If you see the date
and time at the bottom of the screen, they will be recorded on tape. You
probably don't want this.

Opening viewfinder

To open the viewfinder for cleaning or low-angle shots, press the release latch, and pivot the viewfinder up on its hinges.

To remove dust, gently blow with Dust-Off. Smudges may be removed with a microfibre cloth.

Do NOT use lens fluid or solvents. Some of the elements are plastic and may be damaged

Playback

To play tapes back in the camcorder, set the **CAMERA-VTR** switch to **VTR**.

Open the small plastic door on top of the camera to access the VTR control panel.

Custom Preset

Pushing the **CUSTOM PRESET** switch up displays the menu of settings that can be customized and saved for the duration of a production (or longer).

To use it, the menu setting CP SET: ON must be selected.

As with the DSR-PD150, you can control:

Color Level (saturation), Image Sharpness, White Balance shift, and Auto Gain Control Limit.

DSR-300A

The DSR-300A is the next step up from the DSR-250, providing removable lenses and more features. Like the DSR-250, the DSR-300A camcorder accepts Mini and Standard DVCAM or DV cassettes. Unlike the DSR-250, the DSR-300A does not have a flip-out LCD screen. However, an on-board monitor can easily be connected to the BNC monitor output connector. The DSR-300A is a step up in chip size; it has three 1/2" CCD chips, in a 4:3 format shape. (DSR-250 has 1/3" chips.) The DSR-300A uses 1/2" format lenses.

The main difference between this camera, and its more expensive DSR-500WS sibling, is the size and shape of the three chips. The DSR-500WS has 2/3" chips that are native 16:9 in shape.

This camera's price point, for a camcorder with interchangeable 1/2" lenses, makes it attractive for news, television and high-end corporate users who will shooting in 4:3 format, do not need a 16:9 option (there is no 16:9 menu setting), and don't need the higher sensitivity of the CCDs and other advanced features of the DSR-500WS.

Remember that if you see an advertised price that's too good to be true, an earlier model, DSR-300, does not have the i.Link connection.

Many of the features, functions and controls of the DSR-300A are the same as the DSR-500WS, which is explained in the next chapter.

Electrical contacts inside the lens mount mean that you don't have a lens cable to worry about on similarly-equipped lenses.

Sony's DynaLatitude Function adjusts the contrast of the pixels, and the Skin Detail Function controls the area of detail by using a cursor on the viewfinder screen and then pushing the Skin Set button. Black Stretch/Compress Function variably adjusts contrast in the black area of the picture.

EZ Focus opens the lens iris for critical focus. When the iris is opened, the shutter speed is automatically increased to maintain correct exposure. EZ Focus turns off while recording. There is also an EZ Mode autopilot control, which can be customized to user settings. Clear Scan is used to shoot computer monitors by selecting one of 183 shutter speeds that match the scanning frequency of the computer display.

What does the DSR-500WS have that justifies its major jump in price over the DSR-300A? The DSR-500WS has 2/3" CCDs in native 16:9 format (the DSR-300A has 1/2" CCDs in 4:3 format). The DSR-500WS has user files, SetupNavi and some other sophisticated high-end features.

The major, noticeable difference is visible on the switch panel of the DSR-300A: the **MATRIX** switch. It kind of reminds me of the special effect from the movie of the same name, freezing action suspended in mid air while dollying around it— but instead, it provides a helpful choice of color corrections:

> **STD** is the default for normal color
> **FL** corrects the green out of fluorescents
> **H.SAT** adds more saturation to colors.

The next chapter explains the DSR-500WS—but use it as a Jump Start for the DSR-300A as well.

DSR-500WS

This is the current diva of DVCAM, the king of the camcorders, the one with the most buttons to push, the most adjustments to make, the most control over image, interface, output and information. There are enough features and adjustments to fill another book, which will depend on reader clamoring. Since the intent of this book is to introduce DVCAM and not weigh more than the camera itself, I hope to be forgiven for not explaining every switch and knob in the same painful detail provided earlier.

Sony's DSR-500WS camcorder is intended for independent features, television, news, and high-end corporate users. The camera will be familiar to professionals who have shot Betacam SP, Digital Betacam or HD. The path from DSR-PD150 or DSR-250 will also be relatively painless, since many of the features are similar. The DSR-500WS uses the same 1.5-inch black and white viewfinder and battery system as the 250.

The DSR-500WS weighs around 14 lbs (6.3 kg) with its interchangeable zoom lens, viewfinder, tape, lithium-ion battery and microphone.

Its three 2/3" CCD chips are shaped in a "native" 16:9 format, so shooting widescreen is not compromised by avoiding the top and bottom of conventional 4:3 chips.

When shooting in 4:3 format, the left and right sides of the wide chip are not used.

TruEye, DynaLatitude

TruEye is a proprietary way in which the digital signal is processed. The video information, after leaving the CCD chips, is managed at three levels—brightness, hue and saturation—in a manner similar to the way the human eye works. This renders images with improved contrast and truer hues and color. Highlight detail is better retained, and shadow areas have more definition.

DynaLatitude takes contrast management a step further. Since the exposure range of video has a limited dynamic range, DynaLatitude selectively manages the contrast of each pixel.

Skin Detail

Activate the Area Detect Cursor in the viewfinder by sliding the **SKIN DTL** switch ON. Push the **SKIN SET** button, and the effect is similar to a cosmetic diffusion filter in the facial areas only. All other areas remain sharp. The camera knows how to do this by softening only areas designated by skin color. Other colors escape uncorrected. The color range of the Skin Detail active area and Skin Detail level can be set from the viewfinder menu.

Black Stretch and Compress

Contrast in the black area of the image can be variably adjusted using the Black Stretch/Compress Control function. Black Stretch emphasizes contrast in the dark area, while Black Compress enhances or deepens darkness.

Filter Wheel

The DSR-500WS has four built-in filters: 3200 K/3000 K (switchable via the viewfinder menu), 5600 K, 5600 K + 1/8 (-3 stops) and 5600 K + 1/64 (-6 stops).

Wireless Mic

A wireless receiver case has been developed specifically to accommodate the Sony WRR-855A Wireless Receiver, using a CA-WR855 Camera Adaptor.

The Sony CA-WR855 Camera Adapter attaches directly to the DSR-500WS via a V-shoe attachment and a direct audio/power connection interface.

A Lithium-ion battery can also be directly attached to the rear panel of the CA-WR855 via the V-shoe attachment. This allows easy battery replacement even when the WRR-855A is mounted.

Setup Data Management

Camera Setup Files — Eight Setup Files

The DSR-500WS has a Viewfinder Menu System, controlled by a jog wheel similar to the ones found on all other DVCAM cameras. When the **SETUP** switch is set to the **FILE** position, a total of eight setup files can be used with the dedicated Viewfinder Menu System. Five factory Preset Files, programmed by Sony, accommodate the most common lighting situations, such as STANDARD, HIGH SATURATION and FLUORESCENT. Three User Files let you customize settings for different conditions—and then save them in camercorder's memory.

SetupNavi — Camera Setup File Storage

The DSR-500WS Camcorder uses the SetupNavi function to store the User Files or Factory Preset Files of the DSR-500WS directly onto VAUX (Video Auxiliary) data territory of the DVCAM cassette tape. The data can be stored to and recalled from the DVCAM tape by using the VF Menu System.

SetupLog — Automatic Recording of Camera Data

The most important DSR-500WS settings for every shot are automatically recorded onto the VAUX area of DVCAM cassette tapes. This is called the SetupLog function. It is helpful when a shot has to be re-done, and also serves as a valuable log for checking how a particular shot was achieved.

Dual Zebra

The DSR-500WS has two zebra patterns: ZEBRA 1 and ZEBRA 2. ZEBRA 1 can be set anywhere from 70 IRE to 90 IRE, in 1 IRE steps. ZEBRA 2 provides a zebra pattern in any area with more than 100% video level.

EZ Mode

The camera can quickly be put on autopilot by pressing the **EZ MODE** button. There are two EZ Modes: STANDARD or CUSTOM. Standard is the factory auto-everything setting. With CUSTOM EZ Mode, you can preordain camcorder settings from a menu.

EZ Focus

EZ FOCUS helps you focus precisely by opening the lens to its maximum aperture before the camcorder is rolling. To compensate for this, the electronic shutter is automatically set to reduce the amount of incoming light—otherwise it would be too bright. When you push the Record/VTR button, EZ Focus ceases, the lens iris stops down to the correct exposure, and the shutter goes back to normal.

ClipLink

The ClipLink system is a shooting information and image management system integrated in high-end DVCAM products from cameras to editing equipment. ClipLink is available on the DSR-300A and DSR-500WS camcorders, DSR-85, 1500, 1600, 1800 and 2000 VTRs, and EditStation ES-7, ES-3.

ClipLink generates data automatically while shooting. Index Pictures, which are thumbnails of the beginning of each shot, are recorded on the DVCAM tape, in a specially designated area. Shot information useful for editing and logging is stored on the 16K nonvolatile cassette memory chip: reel number, scene number, take number, time code of the MARK IN/MARK OUT point, and OK/NG status.

ClipLink data can be uploaded to a Sony EditStation system from DVCAM VTRs, and streamlines the job of loading all the shots on tape.

16:9 ID Pulse

When shooting in 16:9 format, the DSR-500WS records a wide aspect ID pulse signal onto tape.

Power

The DSR-500WS camera runs off 12 volts DC. Drawing 24 watts, a fully-charged BP-L60A battery pack will last for a little more than 2 hours. A fully charged BP-L90A lasts just under 6 hours.

DSR-500WS Camera Views

Front

Mic

Viewfinder display on/off

Tally light

XLR Mic input w/ +48v powering

Viewfinder connector

Shuttle Shot adjustment

Attached zoom

Index marker

Audio level control

Start/Stop switch

White balance
Black balance

Rear

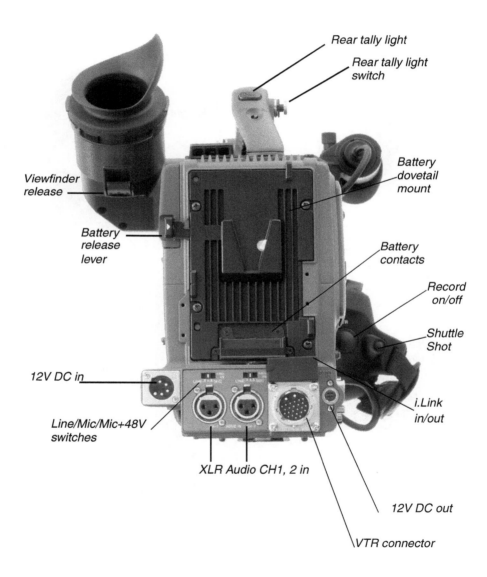

Rear tally light

Rear tally light switch

Viewfinder release

Battery dovetail mount

Battery release lever

Battery contacts

Record on/off

Shuttle Shot

12V DC in

i.Link in/out

Line/Mic/Mic+48V switches

XLR Audio CH1, 2 in

12V DC out

VTR connector

Camera Left

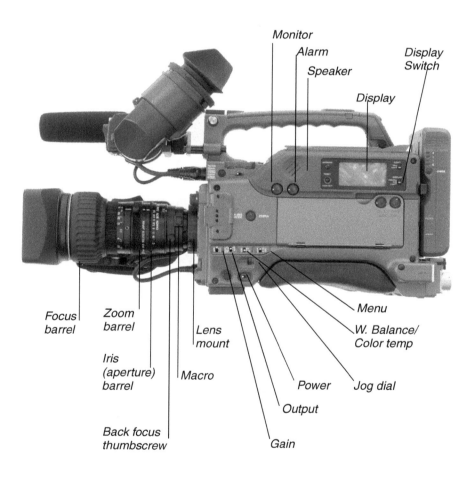

Monitor

Alarm

Speaker

Display Switch

Display

Focus barrel

Zoom barrel

Lens mount

Iris (aperture) barrel

Macro

Back focus thumbscrew

Gain

Output

Power

Jog dial

Menu

W. Balance/ Color temp

Camera Right

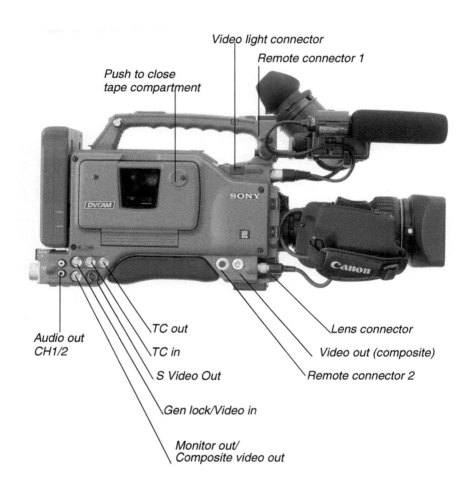

Video light connector

Remote connector 1

Push to close
tape compartment

Audio out
CH1/2

TC out

TC in

S Video Out

Gen lock/Video in

Monitor out/
Composite video out

Lens connector

Video out (composite)

Remote connector 2

DSR-500WS Jump Start

Power and Viewfinder

Users of the DSR-250 who have stepped up to the DSR-500WS will be happy to see the familiar high-end DXF-801/801 CE viewfinder. The DSR-500WS uses the same batteries and viewfinder as the DSR-250. It takes about 2 hours to charge a BP-L60A battery. The LED status on the charger blinks green when it's about 80% charged, and glows a steady green at 100%. WC will ensure that the first shot of the movie takes at least two hours to light, while his batteries are charging.

Select the Lens

The DSR-500WS doesn't come with lens or batteries. They are purchased separately, and hopefully, concurrently.

The lens at right is Canon's YJ18x9B KRS. Lens nomenclature is a mouthful of letters and numbers; here's what they mean on this one:

- YJ is a professional 2/3" lens

- 18x is the zoom ratio, as in 18:1.

- 9 is the focal length at the wide end of the lens.

- B means it's designed for a 3-chip camera (with beamslitter) as opposed to a single chip.

- K indicates the lens doesn't have a built-in doubler (2x tele extender).

- R means the zoom is motorized (with switch to manual), and the focus is manual.

- S means the iris is motorized (with a switch to manual).

In the film world, this lens would be called a 9-162mm F1.8 Zoom with servo zoom and iris, collimated for 3-color beamsplitter. Maybe the lens manufacturers think film people didn't do as well in math class. Math was not my best subject; I can understand 9-162 faster than 18x9.

Lens choices

The Canon 18x9 (9-162mm) is a long telephoto zoom lens. It is good for extreme close-ups far away, ideal for sports, nature, and tripod-mounted shooting. It can focus to 3' (.9m).

For hand-held work, you'll might want to have a wider lens, to get in closer and wider to your subject.

Documentary, news and other hand-held shooters benefit from lenses like Canon's Y12x6.5B KRS lens, which is a 6.5-78mm f2.0/2.6 zoom. It focuses closer than the 18:9 lens—to 1.3' (.4m).

In the ideal camcorder package, we'd own both lenses; but usually we have to make a choice between a short-wide zoom and a longer one.

Fujinon also makes excellent zoom lenses, described in the lens section of this book.

Lens Flange

Be sure the lens flange is clean—free of grease and grit. Clean it with a Kimwipe or denatured alcohol swab.

The optical elements (front and rear) should be cleaned with a microfibre cloth.

The locating pin faces the 12 o'clock position when mounting on the camera.

Remove Lens Cavity Cap on Camera

Use the lens mount lever to rotate the bayonet mount counter-clockwise to loosen.

Remove the cavity cap.

Mount Lens

Insert the lens, locating pin up. Jiggle the lens slightly to be sure it is securely in position. At the same time, rotate the lens mount with your other hand, clockwise to lock.

Remember: Clock(wise) to Lock.

Plug in Lens Cable

The servo motors built into the zoom handgrip of the lens are powered through the cable that plugs into the camera's **LENS** receptacle.

DSR-300A

DSR-300A lens mount has contacts on the lens flange, so some lenses for this camera do not have lens cables.

Arrow on plug faces out. It's hard to see: a drop of white nail polish helps.

Attach Viewfinder and Microphone

The viewfinder is the same as the DSR-250. It plugs into the VF receptacle on the camera body.

Plug the microphone that comes with the camcorder into the 3-pin XLR receptacle at the front.

Set **PEAKING**, **CONTRAST** and **BRIGHT**(ness) to their default 12 o'clock positions.

Switch **DISPLAY ON** and **TALLY LOW**.

DISPLAY OFF turns off viewfinder information. **TALLY** refers to the red light in front.

Attach Battery

As with the DSR-250, the battery attaches to the dovetail at the back of the camera. Align the arrows, and slide down until you hear a click.

To remove the battery, release the locking lever, and lift up.

Behind the Gray Door

Open the Camera Left Control Door.

Set the following slide switches:

CH1 and **CH2**
AUDIO SELECT: AUTO

AUDIO IN: FRONT

MONITOR SELECT: MIX

REGEN (Timecode)

R-RUN (Record Run)

Install Backup Battery

A 3 Volt CR3032 lithium battery backs up camera data and stored setup files for 1 to 2 years.

Be sure it's installed behind the black **LITHIUM BATT** door.

Power Camera On

Turn the Main **POWER** Switch **ON**

Set the Main control switches above it as follows:

GAIN: LOW

OUTPUT: CAM/DL
(DynaLatitude)

W. BAL: PRE (Preset)

MENU: middle position

Set Up Lens

Adjust Back Focus

Still and motion picture lenses do not have back focus adjustment knobs. Instead, they use very thin metal and foil shims to adjust the flange to image plane distance by moving the rear lens element forward or back relative to the rear lens mount. As mentioned earlier, back focus adjustment isn't really necessary on DVCAM equipment, because the prism and chips are very securely mounted and stable, compared with the tubes of early video cameras. Most lens technicians would prefer if the back focus of most video lenses were not so easily field adjustable—being so easy to adjust, they are also easy to come undone. So we have to adjust back focus, and check it every time the camera has been jostled or shipped.

Adjusting back focus begins by mounting the camera on a tripod.

1. Set up a Siemens Star test target about 6' (2m) from the front of the lens. There's a copy of one at the end of this book.

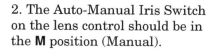

2. The Auto-Manual Iris Switch on the lens control should be in the **M** position (Manual).

(Note that **A** is for Automatic iris control, and the **IRIS** button sets the iris automatically while in Manual. This can be helpful when shooting for a quick-fix on exposure.)

3. Open the lens iris (aperture) all the way—F1.8 on this lens.

4. Zoom all the way in on the Siemens Star—full telephoto, 162mm.

5. Focus until the chart is sharpest. Siemens Stars are used because they tend to "snap" in or out of focus in the eyepiece.

6. Now, zoom out to full wide— 9mm.

7. Loosen the **F.B.** (Flange Back Focus) thumbscrew.

8. Gently rotate the **F.B.** back focus ring until the wide image is sharpest. Do not touch the front focus element. Tighten the thumbscrew.

9. Zoom all the way in to 162mm again. Is the chart still sharp? It should be. If not, repeat the procedure.

10. Buy a roll of 1/16" or 1/8" Chart Tape (Letraline). Place a strip on the back focus ring, and use a Sharpie Fine Point marker to make an index mark for the back focus position.

You might also consider a piece of black electrical tape to cover the knob and ring, preventing accidental loosening on the job.

Set up Lens for Follow Focus

A camera assistant can set up the lens for pulling focus by using Chart Tape on the focus barrel, as shown in the picture above right. The example shows how you might indicate an actor walking from 7' to 4' in front of the camera.

When focusing by tape measure, set up the lens in advance with exact focus index marks. You'll notice that the lens does not have lines to indicate exact focus points. Attach the strip of drafting tape to the barrel.

Set up your Siemens Star chart about 3 feet from the tripod-mounted camera.

The focal plane is not indicated on the camera body—but the front carrying strap screw is close enough, and serves as a good ground-zero over which to loop the end of our tape measure.

Measure out exactly 3', and re-position the Siemens Star focus chart there. Focus the lens.

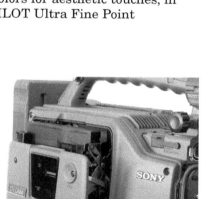

Draw a line on the focus barrel Chart Tape with your Sharpie Fine Point marker as an exact witness mark for 3'. Repeat this procedure for 4, 5, 6, 8, 10, 12, and 20 feet.

Finally, check whether the lens focuses past infinity (some do). If it does, mark where infinity should be.

Letraset "Letraline" works very well: matte finish, easy to write on, 3/16" wide, very thin, comes in a multitude of colors for aesthetic touches, in handy plastic dispensers. For marking: PILOT Ultra Fine Point Permanent Marker.

Load Tape

The DSR-500WS accepts Standard and Mini DVCAM tapes (as well as DV).

Press the EJECT button on top of the camera. (The Main Power Switch has to be **ON**).

Insert the cassette all the way into the chamber, and close the cover by pushing in AND up.

If you see the words "CLIP CONT?" flashing in the viewfinder, push the **ClipLink CONTINUE** button under the Camera Right control panel.

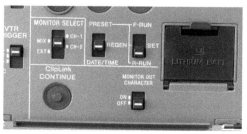

This means the tape has already been used, and ClipLink is active. The camera will find the end of the last-recorded scene and its associated timecode and Cliplink information.

Filter Wheel

Turn the **FILTER** dial at the front of the camera to coincide with the ambient light in which you're shooting:

1. 3200°K (Tungsten)

2. 5600°K + 1/8ND (Daylight 85 with a 3-stop ND.9 gray filter)

3. 5600°K (Daylight 85 filter)

4. 5600°K + 1/64ND (Daylight 85 with a 6 stop ND1.5 gray filter)

EZ Mode

Push the **EZ MODE** button to begin immediately on Auto Pilot: with fully automatic exposure and white balance.

All you have to do is aim, focus and press the record button.

Lens Controls

To start and stop recording, there are two **VTR** buttons: in the thumb position of the handgrip and at the front of the camera body.

The zoom motor is controlled by the Tele and Wide rocker switch.

To switch to Manual zoom, there's a **SERVO-MANUAL** switch at the bottom of the handgrip.

The **RETURN** button on top plays back the last 2 to 10 seconds of your last take, depending on how long you hold the button down.

The **S** (Shuttle Shot) button, next to the **VTR** button, zaps the zoom in for quick focus checks. The amount of zooming is adjusted with the **+-** dial at the front of the handgrip.

Advanced Viewfinder Menu

At this point, WC, the World's Worst Cameraman, could be shooting by now. However, because of previous misadventures, he is always looking over his shoulder, worried about worst-case scenarios. He wants to make sure the cameraman whom he replaced hasn't previously programmed the DSR-500WS with weird settings, as insurance against just such job-replacement scenarios as are evolving today.

Turn **EZ MODE** off (the red LEDs extinguish).

Turn the Main **POWER** Switch **OFF**.

To access the Advanced Menu, Push the **MENU** dial in, and at the same time, turn the camera **POWER** switch **ON**.

Reset Defaults

You'll see the "1" of "PAGE 1" blinking in the viewfinder. Press the **MENU** jog dial. Turn the **MENU** jog dial to scroll down to "ALL RESET." Press the dial. Press the jog dial again to confirm "SURE?" You'll see the confirmation "ALL RESET OK!"

Let's change two defaults before exiting:

Set 16:9 and 4:3 Framelines

No matter how beautiful our composition may be in widescreen 16:9 format, the sad reality is that, after editing, the left and right edges will be chopped off on the majority of TV sets around the world, which are 4:3. Therefore, I find it helpful to include a 4:3 frameline in the viewfinder. Despite the slight distraction, it's better than the embarrassment of seeing missing vital parts later on.

Assuming the cursor is still resting at "ALL RESET OK," turn the jog dial to scroll back up to the text "PAGE 1." Press the dial. The page number blinks. Turn the dial to go to "PAGE 4."

Set "MARKER" to "CENT," which gives you a crosshair in the center of the frame.

Set "LIMITS" to "4:3," which puts a 4:3 frameline inside the 16:9 frame.

Let's change one other default:

Move 16:9/4:3 to Basic Menu

It's easier to change from 16:9 to 4:3 in the Basic Menu. Go to "PAGE 9." Scroll down to "MENU MODE," and change it to "MENU MODE 2." Exit the advanced viewfinder menu.

Basic Menu

The Basic Menu is displayed in the viewfinder by pressing the **MENU** switch down.

As with the Advanced Menu, selections are changed by turning the **MENU** jog wheel, and are selected by pressing it in.

The Basic Menu gives us control over exposure shift, detail level, black master pedestal, black stretch, shutter speeds, skin detail, DynaLatitude Level, Color Temperature shift and so on.

Press the **MENU** switch up to turn the menu display **OFF**.

Momentarily pressing the **MENU** switch up will show the status of the Basic Menu items.

Shutter Speed

The Basic Menu offers choices of shutter speeds only if the **SHUTTER** switch at the front of the camera is **ON**.

The choices for NTSC models are: 1/100, 1/250, 1/500, 1/1000, 1/2000 of a second. In addition, CLS (Clear Scan) provides a selection of vertical scan frequencies from 50.3 Hz to 201.4 Hz, to eliminate roll-bars and flicker on computer and television monitors.

Black Balance

When the camera is first used, when temperatures have changed drastically, and from time to time, set the camera's black balance. With the power on, press the switch down to **BLK**.

Adjustment takes a few seconds.

White Balance

If you decide not to use the Preset White Balance with the 4-filter wheel, the camera can remember two additional white balance settings for up to 10 years.

Let's say we're shooting a feature. On this particular day, we're bouncing back and forth between an interior at a K-Mart, lit with practical, overhead fluorescents, and a location living room, lit with HMI lights coming through the windows.

Nothing in the Preset filter selection would properly remove the sickly green tinge of the fluorescents, and we don't have time or budget to replace all the units with color-correct Kinoflos.

The living room interior could be filtered at 5600°K—but the HMIs are off-temperature, more like 4500°K by the time they are diffused with 216. The producer got a good deal on used bulbs, so of course, they have a substantial amount of green, and the Minus-Green gel has mysteriously disappeared.

This is a great situation in which to take advantage of the **W. BAL A** and **B** switch.

You might want to use **A** for K-Mart and **B** for the living room.

1.   Let's set A first: slide the switch to **W.BAL: A**

2.   Aim the camera at a white card that is lit by the key light.

3.   Push the **WHT-BLK** switch on the front of the camera up to White, and release.

4.   After about a second, the viewfinder displays "AUTO WHITE OK," along with the color temperature of the light. Not bad—you get a free color temper-ature meter with this camera.

5.   Set the **W.BAL: B** switch the same way.

6.   You can now toggle between the two settings.

Be sure to reset white balance if you think the lights are changing or color is drifting. Of course, don't negate all your best efforts to light the scene with an interesting straw gel on the lamps, only to reduce it to neutral white by re-setting white balance.

ATW Auto Tracing White Balance

Pushing EZ MODE activates ATW. But you can also use ATW from outside EZ MODE.

Color Bars

To record bars and tone on a new tape, set the **OUTPUT** switch to **BARS**.

CAM: DL, CDD+

Switch to **CAM DL** when you're ready to record. DL is DynaLatitude, for normal contrast. DCC+ is Dynamic Contrast Control Plus, for highly saturated or high contrast situations—for example, a dimly-lit bar scene, with a large window in the background through which we want to see.

Setting User Bits

At the start of a new cassette, reset User Bits first.

1. Slide the DISPLAY switch to U-BIT.

2. Slide **PRESET-REGEN-DATE/TIME** (left timecode switch) to **PRESET**.

3. Slide **F-RUN-SET-R-RUN** (right timecode switch) to **SET**.

4. The left digit is the camera's display panel blinks.

5. Use the **ADVANCE** button to change the digit.

6. Use the **SHIFT** button to move one digit to the right.

7. Slide the timecode switches back to **REGEN** and **R-RUN** to begin immediately, or proceed to setting timecode.

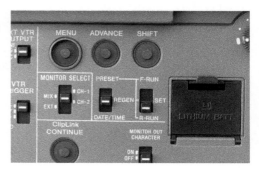

Setting Timecode

1. To reset timecode, slide the **DISPLAY** switch to **TC**.

2. Slide **PRESET-REGEN-DATE/ TIME** (left timecode switch) to **PRESET**.

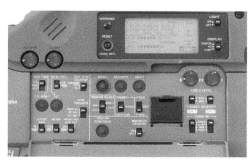

3. Slide **F-RUN-SET-R-RUN** (right timecode switch) to **SET**.

4. The left digit is the camera's display panel blinks.

5. Press the RESET button for 00:00:00:00, or,

6. Use the **ADVANCE** button to change the digit.

7. Use the **SHIFT** button to move one digit to the right.

8. Slide the timecode switches back to **REGEN** and **R-RUN** when you're finished.

VTR Menu

One more menu to navigate. Officially, it's called the VTR Menu, because it mainly adjusts how things are recorded on tape: date, time, frame mode, audio mode and some other non-VTR incidentals like hours of operation.

Set Date

1. Push the **MENU** button

2. Menu number "101" blinks

3. Push **SHIFT** to see the year blinking.

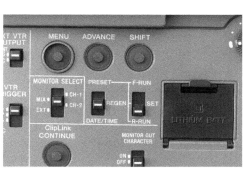

4. Push **ADVANCE** to get the correct year.

5. Push **SHIFT** to see the current month blinking. Set it with the **ADVANCE** button.

6. Push **SHIFT** to see the current date. Set it with the **ADVANCE** button.

7. Continue with the current time.

8. Push **MENU** to accept your selection and return to the display of time-code.

Set DF/NDF

Here's a simplified explanation of the two kinds of NTSC timecode values:

Drop Frame is basically the same as real time. But it skips 2 frame counts here and there to correct for the difference between 29.97 and 30 fps.

Non Drop Frame doesn't do any arithmetic tricks, but timecode gradually increases relative to real time.

Most editors suggest using Drop Frame for broadcast projects, and Non Drop Frame for shows destined to be printed to film.

Footage shot on film and transferred to tape by telecine is usually Non Drop Frame. If you're going to cut the video material in with the film-to-tape footage, shoot in Non Drop Frame mode.

1. Set DF/NDF from the VCR Menu.

    1. Push the **MENU** button.

    2. Menu number "101" blinks.

    3. Push **ADVANCE** to go to menu number "204".

    4. Push **SHIFT**, and select "dF" or "ndF."

    5. Push **MENU** to exit.

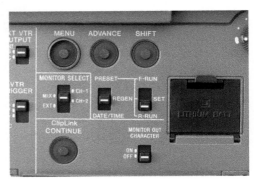

ClipLink

ClipLink uses the DVCAM cassette's16K internal memory chip to log scene number, timecode and NG takes. With an additional board (DSBK-3011A), index picture thumbnails of each scene can be recorded to tape. ClipLink automates shot logging on VTRs and edit systems so designed.

To activate ClipLink, push the Camcorder's VTR **MENU** switch, and advance to menu page "211". Select "on" to activate ClipLink.

If a cassette is rewound, played or ejected while in ClipLink mode, you are prompted to push the **ClipLink CONTINUE** button. This searches for the last recorded scene on the tape, and cues it up for recording—similar to END SEARCH.

Common Features: All Models

Focus and Auto Focus

Autofocus

Otto Focus is the little camera assistant living inside your camcorder, who keeps everything in focus. When he sleeps, a special circuit takes over that analyzes the contrast of the scene. A picture that is in focus has more contrast than when it is out of focus. Check it out with a reflex still camera. Look at a black area next to a white area. As you turn the focus barrel to put the image out of focus, the black area starts looking gray. Anyway, the camcorder checks the scene many times a second, and sends its commands to a miniature servo motor in the lens assembly.

DSR-PD100A, PD150, 250

The Auto Focus on Sony camcorders is fast and usually very accurate. Sometimes it does a better job than your eye. Auto Focus works by taking advantage of an optical theory: a scene has the most contrast (darkest blacks, whitest whites) when it is in focus, and less contrast when it is out of focus. Auto Focus is great—until your interviewee or actor bends down to retrieve the notes that just fell onto the ground. The camcorder lens jumps to the next distant object, and then may hunt back and forth for the speaker, even after he or she is back in frame.

DSR-PD100A

manual focus ring

Furthermore, Auto Focus can be fooled when shooting scenes with little contrast (sky, walls, ocean, snow), or scenes with very low light levels. Use Manual Focus as often as possible when doing dramatic work, or scenes under your control—in other words, shots that can be repeated again.

DSR-PD150

Slide the focus selector to **MANUAL** position. An icon of a hand with the letter "F" appears in the viewfinder or on the LCD screen to indicate you are in manual focus mode.

manual zoom ring

The best way to assure correct focus is to zoom in all the way, turn the lens focus barrel until the image appears sharp, and then zoom out to whatever focal length you like. The image will stay sharp throughout the zoom range.

Sliding the focus selector momentarily down to **INFINITY** can be helpful to reset focus when shooting landscapes. An icon of mountains appears in the finder.

Press the **PUSH AUTO** button momentarily to get a quick automatic focus lock on a subject.

Slide the selector back to **AUTO** to get out of manual focus mode.

Minimum Focus and Field of View

DSR-PD100A

With the lens zoomed in "tight" (T), the closest you can focus is about 30 inches from the front of the lens, which will cover an area (called field of view) that is about 2 1/2" wide x 1 3/4" high.

With the lens zoomed out (W), you can focus to about 1/2 inch from the front element, with a field of view about 1" high x 1 1/2" wide.

So, to get a gorgeous macro shot of that tarantula sitting on your pillow, you'll have to go in close and wide.

DSR-PD150

Minimum focus is about 32 inches from front of lens, with a field of view about 3" wide x 2" high.

Zoom

DSR-PD100A, PD150, 250

Remember your audience: don't make them suffer through too many zooms. Most of us zoom too often.

Try to feather the starts and stops of your zoom as gracefully as possible by using a delicate touch on the zoom rocker control.

The DSR-PD100A does not have manual zoom capability. The DSR-PD150 and DSR-250 have a zoom ring on the lens to zoom by hand.

When the camcorder is on a tripod, use a remote zoom control. It plugs into the LANC receptacle under the rubber cover on the forward camera right side.

Varizoom and Coolzoom are two excellent remote zoom controls.

DSR-300A, 500WS

Zoom controls made by the lens manufacturer or Microforce plug into the remote control connector under the lens

remote
zoom
control
connector

White Balance

The human eye is very tricky. It can be tricked into thinking that a series of flashing images is really continuous. That is why televisions, computer monitors or films projected in movie theatres appear not to flicker after a while. It's called persistence of vision. The longer you look at something, the more your eye and brain adapt.

Try adjusting your computer monitor to different refresh rates. You'll notice flicker, even at 60 Hz. But soon you adapt, and the flicker seems to disappear.

Try another experiment with your eye's "white balance." Turn on a lamp with a standard tungsten filament bulb. Now, look at the sky outside for a couple of minutes. Then, look at the lamp or the wall behind it. It will appear orange-yellow. After a couple of minutes, however, the lamp will appear normal and neutral in color.

The color of light is measured in degrees Kelvin. Daylight averages around 5600 degrees. Household light bulbs are around 3000 degrees. Quartz and tungsten bulbs for film and video lights are 3200°.

And HMI lights are daylight balanced 5600°. It's a good idea to buy a color temperature meter when you get into lighting, to keep the different units consistent. Bulbs have a habit of shifting color temperature as they get old. HMIs in particular can look green or magenta, and can be corrected with gels.

To check color temperature, I like to use the Minolta Color Meter IIIF.

When you buy still film, you have a choice of tungsten or daylight-balanced film. Film is not as clever in adapting as your eye. Neither are video cameras. You have to tell them something about the lighting conditions.

The camcorder has four white balance settings: manual, indoor, outdoor and auto.

The camcorder defaults to automatic white balance when the **AUTO LOCK** switch is in the **AUTO** position.

Setting White Balance

1. To set white balance yourself, slide the **AUTO LOCK** switch to the middle position.

2. Press the **WHT BAL** button at the back of the camcorder.

3. Rotate the jog dial to choose one of three white balance modes: manual, daylight or tungsten. You will see an icon depicting the mode on the middle left of the viewfinder or LCD screen.

Manual White Balance

This is the setting to use for consistent color in studio lighting, as well as correcting fluorescents or sodium vapor lamps that tend to look green. Manual mode also helps compensate for off-color HMI lights. To set Manual White Balance, hold a white showcard, foamcore, or piece of white paper in front of the camcorder. Zoom in to fill the frame with white. Or aim at a white wall.

Press the control dial momentarily. You do not have to keep pressing on it.

The manual icon will flash quickly. When it stops flashing, manual white balance has been set, and will remain stored in the camcorder's memory for as long as you have power, and for an additional hour after the battery is dead or removed.

It's a good idea to use the same white card for the duration of the shoot. If you use different cards with different values of white, the scenes will not match. White balancing this way makes all the whites look white, of course. This could become boring after a while.

What if you want your video to have a warm, amber look? You can shift the color balance of your scenes away from normal by using a white balance reference light, sometimes called a slate light. Keep an inkie or small 3200° unit available to illuminate the white card. Have both accessible for the duration of the shoot. Set your white balance for the card and its reference light. Then gel your lights according to the color shift desired: CTO for a warmer look, CTB for cooler, CTS for an amber-straw tone, chocolate for a sepia tint. Rosco and Lee are two major manufacturers of gels, which are actually made of acetate and other temperature resistant plastics. The word gel comes from the early days of photography, when color control really was done with gelatine.

If you're frugal or pressed for time, you can let the laws of complementary colors work for you. Again, let's say you want a warm, orange look—but you are on such a low budget, you can only afford a couple of tiny gels for the inkie. Experiment with CTB (blue) gels. Try shooting your white card and setting white balance with 1/2 CTB on the inkie. You will be fooling the camera into thinking this extra blue light is actually white. So when the camera "sees" normal tungsten lights, they will appear extra orange, without your having to gel each one.

Remember, the slate light should be the complementary color of what you want things to look like.

What if we want our video to have a cool, blue look? Add CTO (orange) gel to the slate light, and set your white balance for that. The camera is now fooled into shifting everything toward a bluer tone.

Daylight (Outdoor, 5600°K) White Balance

Even though it is called "daylight," the color temperature outside varies throughout the day. At sunrise and sunset it can be as orange as a tungsten light (3200°). A foggy, early morning can be so cool your color temperature meter reads above 12,000°. Be careful to check your image when using this setting.

Tungsten (Indoor, 3200°K) White Balance

Indoor mode is useful when shooting in studios or controlled lighting situations. You can avoid manual white balancing this way. You can also gel your lights, as we described in the manual mode, to shift the color away from normal.

Zebra Stripes and Exposure

Unfortunately, video cameras do not have built-in lightmeters like still cameras and some movie cameras. It would be nice if they did. A simple, center-weighted match-needle or spot-meter electronic display would help maintain consistent exposure.

The problem with relying on our eyepiece to judge scene brightness and contrast is that old problem of how easy it is to fool the human eye. As with white balance, the longer we look at something, the more normal it appears. Also, the eyepiece is pretty small, and not as accurate as a good studio monitor. So we can shoot ten different scenes thinking we are keeping them very consistent. Much to our horror, when we see the ten scenes displayed as thumbnails side by side in our editing room, we notice how easily our eye was fooled.

It's not always practical to lug a studio monitor around in the field. Fortunately, there are two things that can help us maintain consistent exposure.

Zebra stripes quickly show where a scene is over-exposed (too much light).

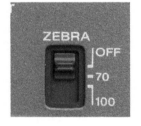

The three-position **ZEBRA** switch is either **OFF**, 70% IRE or **100**% IRE.

The zebra stripes appear as white diagonal zebra lines in the viewfinder or LCD. Obviously, they are not recorded on tape.

At 100%, you'll see stripes over areas of the picture where reflected brightness is equal to or greater than Video 100%, and the 70% setting will display stripes on portions of the scene at 70%.

What this means is that a picture is assigned brightness values of 0 to 100. "How can anything be brighter than white?" you ask. Hold a piece of white foamcore up to a backlit window. Both appear white. But the window is much brighter.

How can something be darker than black? Again, look at the difference between a black showcard and a piece of black felt or velour.

They can be helpful in maintaining consistent whites. Don't try to close down your aperture totally to eliminate the white zebra stripes. A little over-exposure looks good.

Try to remember how much area was covered by stripes in your previous scene. Let's say you were doing a political spot. Your politico is standing against a white wall in Scene 1, a wide shot. In Scene 2, you go in for a close-up or him making a speech. The same wall is in the background. The white level should be the same, with the same amount of zebra stripes.

Determining Effective ASA

Here's a quick and unscientific way to find out the effective ASA of your camcorder, rating it so you can use a lightmeter for consistent look.

DSR-PD150, DSR-250

1. Set the camcorder's **ZEBRA** Pattern to 70 (70%).

2. Turn on Manual exposure (Iris).

3. Set the manual shutter to 1/60.

4. Be sure there is no ND filtration, and the GAIN is 0.

5. Aim the camcorder at a Kodak 18% gray card, or a Caucasian face. They both have almost the same amount of light reflectance.

6. Adjust the lens aperture (iris) until you just start seeing zebra stripes on the 18% gray card or the face. Notice what the f-stop is.

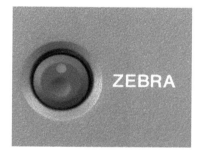

DSR-300A, DSR-500WS:
Set to 70% from Advanced Menu, page 4

7. Pick up your Spectra IVa incident lightmeter. Measure the incident light coming toward the gray card or the face. Aim the globe of the meter toward the camcorder. Do NOT aim the meter toward the card. That would be a reflected reading.

8. Adjust the Spectra meter so its LCD displays 1/60 second and the f-stop you observed on the camcorder. The variable, desired ASA, will now be revealed. I find the Sony DSR-PD150 and DSR-250 are equivalent to 400 ASA. The DSR-PD100A seems to be 250 ASA. The DSR-300A and DSR-500WS are around 250 to 320 ASA.

Manufacturers don't rate the camcorders as if it were film, because there are so many variables of lenses, filters, gain, shutter speeds and look. However, preliminary testing and analysis on a waveform monitor can guide you in determining how you'd like to rate your camcorder. And, of course, when doing high-end work and dramatic features, a waveform monitor is essential.

Lightmeter

Now that you know your ASA, you can check lighting ratios, maintain consistent exposure, and even know when the electronic gain circuitry is going to kick in. Even though your camera says it can record down to 7 Lux, that doesn't mean you shouldt avoid adding some light if you have the time and equipment.

Neutral Density Filters

Neutral density filters are like sunglasses for your camcorder.

ND filters camcorders do not use the same terminology as photographic ND filters. I wish they did. A 1 stop light reduction is ND.3, 2 stops is ND.6, 3 stops is ND.9, 4 stops is ND1.2 and so on.

The ND filter on Sony's DSR-PD100A causes an 84% reduction of light. This approximates an ND.9 filter, which cuts light down by 3 stops.

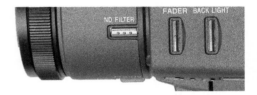

The DSR-PD150 and DSR-250 have a 3-position ND switch, labeled **OFF, 1, 2**.

According to Sony specs, **1** allows 1/4 of the light to reach the CCD, and **2** lets 1/32 of the light reach it.

So, **1** is the photographic equivalent of ND.6, cutting down 2 f-stops of light.

2 is the photographic equivalent of ND1.5, cutting out approximately 5 f-stops.

The filters of the DSR-300A and DSR-500WS are 1/8 (ND.9—3 stops) and 1/64 (ND1.8—6 stops)

Gain

When using manual gain control, 3 db equals 1/2 stop. Anything above 6 db might introduce noise that could be bad for broadcast.

Timelapse

Timelapse is the effect you see in almost every financial and technology company commercial—clouds zipping by at high speed, arrays of satellite dishes re-aiming simultaneously, car headlights blurred into a ribbon of light.

Timelapse is basically an animation technique for live action. By shooting single frames with extra time between them, we are, in essence, compressing a long period of time into a much shorter time. Let's say it takes one hour for a beautiful sunset to occur. It begins with the sun a few degrees above the horizon, and ends as the sky has gradually changed from a multitude of red and pink hues with wispy clouds into a rich purple-blue with just the hint of a glow where earth meets sky.

Now, what if we want to do a title sequence, and show all this in 2 minutes? We need to do a little math. 60 minutes is 3600 seconds. Let's take one shot (one frame) every second. We'll have 3600 exposures. How much real-time is that? Well, our results, even though they were shot at a rate of 1 frame per second, will be played back at 30 frames per second—or 25 frames if we're using PAL. So, we divide 3600 exposures (frames) by 30 frames, and the result is 120 seconds, or two minutes.

Timelapse is a combination of: burst—how many frames are exposed at any given time, interval—how long we wait between bursts, and exposure—combination of aperture and shutter for each frame exposed.

Interval Recording

Few camcorders, the DSR-PD100A included, can do true frame-by-frame timelapse because it is difficult for them to record just one frame. You can approximate the effect using the Interval Recording mode. Think of it more as a surveillance type of mode, like they have in banks. It records a burst as short as 1/2 a second, with intervals as short as 30 seconds, going up to 10 minutes.

To get to Interval Recording mode, press the **MENU** button while the Main Power Switch is turned to **CAMERA.** Turn the jog wheel to the *CAMERA SET* menu, and press to accept the following sequence: *INT. REC - SET - INTERVAL* (choice of *30 SEC, 1, 5, 10 MIN*) - *REC TIME* (choice of .5, 1, 1.5, 2 SEC) and then press **MENU** to accept your choices.

Cut Recording

Cut Recording is the closest most camcorders can come to true Stop Motion. The difference between this mode and Interval Recording is that you control the time between exposures. Each time you push the Record Button, six frames of video are recorded. To get there, in **CAMERA** mode, push **MENU**, and turn the jog wheel to *FRAME REC-ON*, and push the **MENU** button to accept your choice.

Batteries

Rechargable batteries do NOT last forever. Depending on brand and how they were used, you can expect to buy new batteries after about 200 charge-discharge cycles.

DSR-PD100A and DSR-PD150

Sony DSR-PD100A and DSR-PD150 camcorders share the same 7.2 volt Lithium Ion batteries and charger. Batteries are charged while attached to the camera, and the charger doubles as an AC adaptor. Lithium Ion batteries do not have the dreaded "memory effect" of Ni-Cads, which required careful attention to discharging to prolong longevity.

DSR-250

The DSR-250 (along with DSR-300A and DSR-500WS) use 12 volt batteries. The BC-L50 charger (shown here) will charge two Lithium Ion batteries in a couple of hours. You cannot charge batteries attached to the camera.

Two AC Adaptors are available. The external AC-550 plugs into the camera's **DC IN 12V** 4-pin XLR receptacle. The AC-DN1 attaches like an on-board battery.

I don't like AC adaptors because it's so easy for someone to kick out the plug.

Playback

The moment has come to review your masterpiece.

DSR-PD100A and DSR-PD150

On the DSR-PD100A and DSR-PD150, turn the Main Power Switch to VTR.

The VTR panel on top of the camera lights up. Microswitches beneath the rubbery-plastic membrane control the movement of the tape within.

Press **REW** to rewind.

Press **PLAY** first, and then **REW** to rewind and see the picture at the same time.

Press **PLAY** first, and then **FF** to fast forward while watching the picture.

It's easiest to watch on the swing-out LCD screen.

Whatever you do, DO NOT press **REC** and the blank button to its right. That will erase and record over your tape.

DSR-250

On the DSR-250, set the 3-position **MEMORY-CAMERA-VTR** switch to VTR.

The playback controls are on top of the camera under a gray plastic cover.

End Search

The **END SEARCH** button provides a quick way to find the last recorded portion of a tape on the DSR-PD100A, 150 and DSR-250.

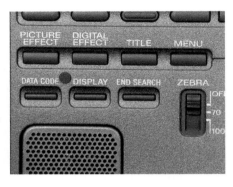

It works with the Main Power Switch set to either **CAMERA** or **VTR**.

It is especially helpful when using DV or DVCAM tapes with cassette memory (you can tell because there's a copper-colored metal strip just below the **SAVE-REC** slider).

Without cassette memory, **END SEARCH** will not work after the tape is ejected from the camcorder.

HOWEVER: I do not recommend relying totally on **END SEARCH**. It will not behave correctly if there is a blank portion between scenes (you popped the tape in and out a couple of times, or reviewed footage in between recording). Therefore, always double check your footage with the **PLAY** button.

Edit Search

Edit Search is a bit tricky—not intuitive, and an easy way to erase footage. It is used to review tape while the Main Power Switch is in **CAMERA** mode on the DSR-PD100A, 150 and DSR-250..

Let's say you're shooting, and want to make sure the last take looks good. Without having to open the LCD screen, you can momentarily push the button of the **EDITSEARCH** control at the top front of the camcorder.

The tape rewinds two seconds, and then plays back the last two seconds on the LCD viewing screen or in the Viewfinder.

But, what if you keep pressing the - button? You see the recorded image while the tape plays back in reverse as long as you hold the button. When you release it, the picture goes "live." If you momentarily push the - button down again, just two seconds will play back. After two seconds, the tape stops, and the picture goes "live" again.

To review in the forward direction, press the + button of **EDITSEARCH.**
You will see recorded tape as long as the button is pushed down.

The danger with all this is that you're in the middle of the tape, with the
Main Power Switch precariously parked on **CAMERA** and ready to record.
Use this function with caution.

So, if you use **EDITSEARCH,** be sure to use the **END SEARCH** control to
make sure you're at the end of the tape, or use the **PLAY** button.

In/Out and Dubbing

Audio and Video Input and Output
connectors lurk beneath the rubber
cover on camera right.

Analog video and audio comes out of
the yellow mini-plug receptacle. Plug
in the special 4-conductor A/V cable
that comes with the camcorder.

At the other end of the cable,
Composite video comes out of the
yellow RCA plug. The red RCA jack is
Audio-Right, and the white one is
Audio-Left.

DSR-PD100A

Plug these connectors into your TV,
monitor or VTR.

S-Video, which separates the video
signal into luminance and
chrominance for higher quality, is
accessed from the S-VIDEO
receptacle on the camcorder. You still
need to use the special A/V cable for
sound, but you can disconnect the
yellow composite video RCA
connector.

DSR-250

These same connectors can be used to dub video onto the tape. Set the
Main Power Switch to VTR, and use the top **REC** controls.

The **DV IN/OUT** receptacle provides both input and output of the digital
video and audio signal. Dubbing from another DVCAM or DV camcorder
or deck is done with one i.LINK cable for both digital video and audio.

The **LANC** receptacle is for edit control. It also provides access to camera
functions for external controls like zoom control and camera start/stop.

i.LINK In/Out

DSR-PD100A and DSR-PD150 camcorders have a 4-pin i.LINK (Firewire) receptacle, labelled **DV IN/OUT**. This is the digital spigot—for digital video and audio data.

The DSR-250 has a 6-pin i.LINK connection at the right rear corner of the camcorder.

The BNC connector to the left is composite video out.

Keying

Images stored on a Memory Stick can be keyed over camcorder images.

M.CHROM (Memory Chromakey): The blue area of a still image on the Memory Stick can be replaced with a picture from the camcorder.

LUMI (Memory Luminance key): The bright part of a still image on the Memory Stick can be replaced by an image from the camcorder.

C.CHROM (Camera Chromakey): A moving picture from the camcorder can be superimposed on a still image from the Memory Stick.When shooting a picture with a blue background, the area of the moving picture will be taken out and the still picture will be shown.

M.Overlap (Memory Overlap): The still image on the Memory Stick can be faded into a moving picture.

Still Photos

There are two ways to use your DVCAM Camcorder as a still camera: grabbing 7 seconds of the frozen image on tape, or capturing the same image on a chewing-gum shaped Memory Stick.

The advantage of shooting stills on tape is that you can capture up to 340 images on one 40-minute DVCAM cassette, using a very cheap form of storage, compared to the relatively expensive Memory Stick. The same tape can be used for both stills and full-motion video, alternately taking stills and shooting video.

The disadvantage of using tape is that you have to wait 7 seconds for each one to be stored. It would be nice if there were a fast mode, perhaps called City Stills, which only records for one second.

The second way to shoot stills is to record the data onto a Memory Stick. The DSR-PD100A, DSR-PD150 and DSR-250 DVCAM camcorders have a Memory Stick slot. The image will be the same size and resolution as one recorded on tape, but is recorded much faster to a flash memory chip.

As of this writing, neither form of still photo capture should make you want to give away your multi-megapixel digital still camera. DVCAM stills are 640x480, producing a 4" wide x 3" high, 160 dpi, 900K BMP bitmap or 65K JPG file.

Progressive or Interlace Scan

Interlace is the normal way we are accustomed to watching video: half the horizontal lines are displayed in one 1/60th of a second, and then the rest of the scan lines are displayed in the next 1/60th second (1/50th second in PAL).

In progressive scanning on the current line of DVCAM camcorders, all the horizontal lines are recorded approximately every 1/15th of a second (NTSC), which means that every field is "printed twice," or duplicated— the equivalent of 15 fps. The camcorder's default setting is Interlace. Incidentally, 24P cameras record every field of every frame just once.

Stills will look sharper when shot in progressive scan mode. Every scan line is employed for every field. Be sure to return to Interlace Mode after the stills are shot. Because I usually forget, or don't have time to switch back and forth, I usually shoot everything in Interlace Mode.

When importing stills from tape to computer, some still capture programs will line-double the image.

To change the scan mode, access the **MENU** while in Standby. You'll see the words "*PROG. SCAN*" appear in the left center of the finder.

Recording Stills

On Tape

It's easy to quickly go between full motion video and stills on tape.

Keep the main power switch in the **CAMERA** position.

1. Push the red record button to start recording video, or...

2. Gently, push down on the **PHOTO** button on top of the camcorder until the image freezes and you see an icon of a still camera and the word *"CAPTURE"* in the upper right of the finder.

3. If you like what you see, push down harder on the **PHOTO** button to begin saving the image to tape. The word *"CAPTURE"* is replaced by seven red dots, that count down to 1. When it's over, the camcorder beeps twice, and goes back into Standby, ready for another still photo or video recording.

4. If you don't like what you see when lightly pressing on the **PHOTO** button, release it, re-compose, and press down lightly again.

5. You can also shoot a still while recording video. While the tape is rolling, simply press down all the way on the **PHOTO** button. The image is frozen for 7 seconds, and then the camcorder goes into standby. Remember—the camcorder records sound during the interminable 7 seconds of grabbing the still, so any comments you have to say will be recorded.

Recording Stills on Memory Stick

Recording to the Memory Stick is very similar to recording to tape.

Set the Main Power Switch to the **MEMORY** position.

If it will not move past the **CAMERA** position, the safety lock-out is engaged.

To record still photos onto the Memory Stick, slide the little safety tab forward (towards the front of the camcorder). Pressing the red record button will no longer work.

To take a still photo, gently push the **PHOTO** button on top of the camcorder.

You will hear the simulated sound of a still camera shutter. This is misleading—do not assume the image has been recorded yet. The word *"CAPTURE"* appears in the upper right of the finder.

To record the image to the Memory Stick, push the **PHOTO** button down all the way. A red bar graph display appears in the upper right. It takes one or two seconds to record to the Memory Stick.

There are three levels of image resolution, displayed in the finder at top center: standard (*STD*), fine (*FINE*) and super fine (*SFN*). The images are recorded as JPEG files. Standard (1/10 compression) files are about 60KB each, Fine (1/6 compression) are about 100KB, and Super Fine (1/3 compression) are about 190 KB. As far as I can tell, the dpi is the same in all three resolutions, and the main difference is in anti-aliasing and some other subtle differences. Use Super Fine whenever possible.

Changing Image Quality

1. Change image quality by accessing the Menu with the Main Power Switch set to **MEMORY**.

2. Go to Memory Stick settings.

3. From Quality, choose Standard (1/10 compression), Fine (1/6 compression), or Super Fine (1/3 compression).

Viewing Stills on Tape

The easiest way to see your stills is to simply play the tape. Since the pictures were recorded for 7 seconds each, it's like a slide show.

The memory chip in the cassette automatically indexes stills by date and time. The Remote Commander (Remote Control) can help you find these pictures. Be sure "*COMMANDER*" and "*CM SEARCH*" are both *ON* in the menu. Then, press SEARCH MODE on the Remote Commander, and press the forward or back arrows.

Viewing Stills on Memory Stick

To review the pictures on the Memory Stick:

1. The Main Power Switch can be in either the **VTR** or **MEMORY** position.

2. Access the Memory Stick control buttons. On the DSR-PD100A or DSR-PD150, they are behind the LCD viewing screen. On the DSR-250, they're next to the audio controls.

3. Push **PLAY**. The still photo most recently shot is displayed on screen.

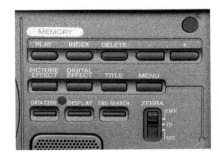

DSR-PD100A

3. Push "**+**" or "**-**" to cycle through the stills stored on the Memory Stick.

4. All kinds of information is displayed at the top of the LCD screen, beginning at the upper left: filename, image resolution, image number out of total image shot, and "*MEMORY PLAY*," in case you've forgotten what you're looking at.

5. Push **INDEX** to see 6 images at a time. Press **+** or **-** to cycle through the index.

6. Press **PLAY** to see a specific photo full-screen.

8. Press **DELETE** to get rid of photos.

The camcorder asks for your blessing.

Press **DELETE** again.

If the images won't go away, eject the Memory Stick, and chances are that the write-protect tab is in the **LOCK** position.

The DSR-PD100A (above right) uses a PCMCIA adapter to hold the Memory Stick.

DSR-PD150 and DSR-250 camcorders accept the Memory Stick directly (see photo at right). To eject, push in, and the stick should pop out.

9. Press the **PLAY** button again to get out of Memory playback and back to live.

Transferring Stills to Computer

There are many places your stills can go: Memory Stick to tape, tape to Memory, and so on. But the most useful function of all is getting a still onto your computer, where it can be ready for email to defenceless relatives and friends, gracing the company's new website, or on the jacket cover of your DVD.

Plug camcorder into Computer

Plug a 4-pin FireWire/IEEE 1394/i.LINK cable into the camcorder's **DV IN/ OUT** receptacle. Remember, there are two kinds of connectors: the small, 4-pin style, and the larger, 6-pin variety.

Plug the other end of the cable into your computer's IEEE 1394 receptacle. You can purchase 4-pin to 6-pin cables and adapters at most computer stores. PC Connection can mail you one overnight.

When all else fails, reboot the computer with the camcorder's main power switch set to **VTR**.

Using Sony DVgate Still

Most Sony laptops and towers come with DVgate Still, a good Windows program for grabbing stills from the DVCAM Camcorder and saving them on the computer.

1. Launch the program (Start-Programs-VAIO-DVgate-DVgate Still).
2. Open all three windows: Control Panel, Monitor and Still. (Click on the Window Menu of the DVgate Still Control Box, and check Monitor and Still)

3. If the camcorder is off, the Control Panel says "OFFLINE." You must turn on the camcorder. Turn the power switch to "VTR;" the Panel now displays "ONLINE."

4. Click on SETUP of the Monitor Window. Go down to SETTINGS. Select High, Medium or Low Resolution. Suggestion: use High Resolution. You can always compress file size later.

5. Control the camcorder with the control panel. Click on the PLAY arrow to begin. Hovering the mouse over the different controls shows a description of the particular buttons.

6. The tape plays back everything you've recorded: stills and full motion video.

7. Click on "CAPTURE" whenever you want to grab a frame. The frame will be displayed in the STILL window.

8. The reason for the 7-second still duration becomes evident when you quickly scan through the tape.

9. To grab a single frame of moving images, click the STEP button, and FREEZE when you get the shot you like.

10. To grab a full second of video—30 frames—click in the Control Panel Window on Settings - Capture - Capture Frames Continuously.

11. But wait. The stills are grabbed, but not saved.

12. To copy a still to the clipboard, find the shot you like in the STILL window by clicking on one of the arrows. Click COPY to save a bitmap image to the clipboard, which then must be pasted into another application.

13. To save images to disk, click on SAVE in the STILL window.

14. Select your destination. Suggestion: keep all your DV stills in a directory called DV Stills. Select the file type.
    A Windows Bitmap (BMP) will be about 900K. JPEG (JPG) files are about 65K and Digital Video Format (DVF) files are about 90K.
I usually save files as bitmaps, and then convert them to TIF files in Photoshop.

If the files are just going on the Internet, I'll save as a smaller JPG file. I avoid GIF files because of limited color depth, and DVF because they don't import easily into other applications.

Downloading Memory Stick Photos

When transferring images recorded on Memory Stick using DVgate Still, the control panel camcorder controls will not work.

View the pictures as described earlier, using **MEMORY PLAY, +** and **-**.

The pictures will appear on the Monitor window, and can be grabbed in the STILL window with the CAPTURE button.

I find very little discernible difference between pictures recorded on DVCAM tape or on Memory Stick.

Sony Smart Capture

Sony Smart Capture is another software application that can be used to get still and moving images onto your computer. Although you cannot control the camcorder from the computer, it offers a quick alternative.

Be sure to set the image size under "OPTIONS:" 640x480, 320x240, 160x120, or 80x60.

Click CAPTURE in the Smart Capture window, and SAVE in the Still Viewer.

The EFFECTS button provides all kinds of gratuitous image adjustments, including sepia, outline, emboss and negative.

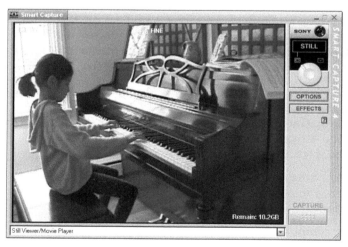

Touching up Your Pictures

Pixels, Dots and DPI

Picture files on your computer are made up of lots of little dots, called pixels. Hold an 8x magnifying glass up to your computer screen. You'll see them. Color pictures are made of red, green and blue pixels, arranged side by side. Black and white photos on a color monitor are still displayed with the same color pixels, but they are blended to look like shades of gray.

When you have an image that measures 640x480, it means the picture has 640 dots going left to right, and 480 dots going from top to bottom. So, a 640x480 pictures consists of 307,200 pixels. Actually, multiply that number by 3 and you get 921,600—since each pixel really has 3 dots: red, green and blue.

When you buy a computer monitor, its display properties are given in pixel count. Monitors from the late 1980s couldn't display anything larger than 640x480 edge to edge. Most monitors now routinely display 1024x768 pixels, and go up to 1600x1200.

But that's just part of the story. The size of each dot also determines resolution and sharpness. Most monitors have a default screen resolution of 72 dots per inch. That means there are 72 pixels arranged side by side for each inch. This is fine for most NTSC video at 640x480.

Let's say our monitor is set at 640x480. A 64 x480 72 dpi video image would take up the entire screen. Let's change the monitor's resolution to 1280x1024. A 640x480 picture with a resolution of 72 dpi (dots per inch) would most likely take up just half of the screen's real estate. But what if we change the resolution to 36 dpi? We'll still have 640 dots going left to right, but they will be spread out farther apart. The picture will now take up the whole screen, but it won't look as sharp because of the space between each pixel.

Now, what if we increase resolution to 144 dpi? The pixels are displayed closer together, making the image look sharper. And, those 640 pixels will take up just 1/4 of the screen. There is a direct correlation between number of pixels, dpi, picture resolution and picture size.

Look at a newspaper photo and a picture from an inkjet printer with a magnifying glass. They're made of similar red, blue and green dots, along with black for extra contrast.

However, dpi on the computer screen does not translate directly into dots on the page. Dots on the page are better measured in LPI, for Lines Per Inch, which are really lines or rows of pixels going across the page.

Printer DPI to LPI

To see how DPI on screen relates to LPI on the page, divide the printer's advertised dots per inch resolution by 16.

DPI / 16 = LPI

So, a 1200 dpi laser printer will yield the following:

1200 / 16 = 75 lines per inch. Aha! That's why photos from your laser print don't look so great.

The pictures in this book are printed at 2400 DPI, so we get 150 lines per inch.

Current inkjet printers are capable of up to 2880 dots per inch, which is 180 lines.

Screen DPI to Printer DPI

The opposite also holds true. Multiply the DPI (pixels per inch) of your photo by 12 to see what the corresponding printer resolution will be. If you have a 96 pixel/inch (96 dpi) image file:

96 Pixels/Inch x 12 = 1152 printer DPI.

So, the picture is not going to look great.

What does this all mean?

When you transfer a still image from the camcorder to your computer, it is usually a BMP bitmap image of 640x480 pixels, 96 pixels/inch (DPI), measuring 6.66 inches wide x 5 inches high, that takes up 900Kb of disk space. If you're lucky enough to have a camcorder that can save stills as JPEG files, they'll take up only 70Kb for the same size image because they compress the file.

Now, we know that a 96 pixel/inch photo isn't going to look very good when printed out. What should we do?

We'll open the picture in an image editing program, and by making it smaller, we'll increase the resolution. Remember, we still have all those pixels to work with. We just need to bunch them closer together.

The smaller you make a picture, the sharper it will look when printed out. By setting a new size of 300 dpi in the lower box will give you good results. Anything larger than 4" x 6" will become grainy. If you just want to send the picture by email, 72 dpi is fine.

Adobe Photoshop

Adobe Photoshop is the industrial strength, industry standard image editor. Some recommended books on Photoshop are: Adobe's *Photoshop Classroom in a Book,* Martin Evening's *Adobe Photoshop 6.0 for Photographers,* and *Photoshop Studio Secrets* by Deke McClelland, Katrin Eismann (Photoshop Diva) et al.

For our one-page Photoshop Lesson, let's adjust image size.

Open your image from the menu with FILE-OPEN.

Click on IMAGE-IMAGE SIZE.

To make your pictures higher in resolution (sharper), but smaller in size, uncheck the RESAMPLE IMAGE box. (Yes, the Constrain commands of PhotoDeluxe are more intuitive). Be sure "Constrain Proportions" is checked—if it's grayed out, but checked, that's fine.

To make pictures smaller and lower resolution for the web, be sure RESAMPLE IMAGE is checked.

Photoshop does its work in layers. To save to a TIF or JPG file, you may have to combine all the layers. Click on LAYER-FLATTEN IMAGE. Then, click on FILE-SAVE AS, and select your file format.

By the way, the picture above measures 1024 x 1535 pixels. This is what is known as a "megapixel" image, and where we're headed in digital photography: more and more pixels.

Audio

The built-in microphones or on-board mini-shotgun mikes that come with most camcorders are fine for ambient sound. However, these on-board mikes can pick up tape transport and zoom motor noise. For serious audio, use a separate microphone. Most professional crews have a sound mixer, whose job it is to aim to microphone, set the levels and monitor the audio. The mixer feeds the camcorder with the audio signal, either with a "hard" wire or a radio mic. Because DVCAM tape records on two tracks, you can split the audio—for example, you can put a lavalier output on the right channel, and a shotgun mic for ambience on the left channel. Popular choices of shotgun (directional) mikes include Sennheiser's MKH-416, ME66 and K6 and Audio-Technica's AT815. Lavalier mikes look like little tie clips, and are plugged directly into the camcorder or sent by radio-transmitted. Popular lavaliers are Sony's ECM-77B and ECM-44B, and Audio-Technica's AT831B.

The DSR-PD100A is the only DVCAM camcorder with built-in stereo microphones, seen in the photo at right just below the SONY logo.

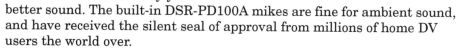

The good news is that built-in microphones are fast, easy to use and always there.

The not-so-bad news is that external mikes invariably yield better sound. The built-in DSR-PD100A mikes are fine for ambient sound, and have received the silent seal of approval from millions of home DV users the world over.

The problem is, built-in microphones picks up motor noise from the camcorder's tape transport, and aren't very selective about cancelling out wind or background noise. If you're far away from your subject, you'll probably hear yourself more clearly than anything else.

So, sticking a microphone on the front of your camcorder is not the best way to record sound. You can do better.

Mini shotgun on DSR-PD100a

Despite the fact that every news camera in the world has an on-board mic, the secret to good sound recording is having another microphone as close to your subject as possible.

On-camera reporters will often hold the microphone. Professional sound engineers use shotgun microphones or booms to position the microphone just out of frame.

DSR-PD150

If the shot is wide or the subject is moving around, a small lavalier microphone, attached to a radio transmitter, will be hidden under the talent's clothing. A radio receiver, which connects directly to the camcorder, is tuned to the same frequency as the radio mic.

Audio Input

On the DSR-PD100A, there are two ways to recorded audio onto tape: using the internal microphone, or plugging an external one into the **MIC** mini plug or XLR connector.

The one pictured at right is the mini plug.

(The Audio/Video receptacle is a line input connection. And, it's a good idea to connect a headset to the headphone terminal to monitor your audio.)

XLR Connector

Professional microphones use 3-pin XLR connectors. The cables are shielded in such a way as to cancel out hum and noise. This is called balanced audio.

The DSR-PD100A has an accessory box that attaches to the "hot shoe" on top of the camera. A microphone plugged into the XLR

connector sends its audio signal through the contacts in the hot shoe to the camcorder and tape.

To attach the accessory box, slide it from front to back, and tighten the knurled ring.

A microphone holder attaches above the accessory box.

Plug the microphone into the XLR receptacle.

The **+48V** switch provides 48 volts at low amperage to power many professional microphones. This is called phantom powering. Turn it **ON** if your mic requires it.

The 3-position **LEVEL** switch on the left should usually be set to the middle **STD** position. If sounds are too loud, slide it to **ATT** (attenuate). If the audio is really faint, slide it to **GAIN**.

It's a good idea to watch the level indicator in the eyepiece. Activate it from the menu.

48K Audio

Be sure to set the Audio Mode to FS48K in the menu settings. This will provide two 48K (16-bit) audio tracks, as opposed to FS32K, which records four tracks at 32K (12-bit).

Split Tracks

Take advantage of both audio tracks. If you're using a single microphone, get an audio splitter and feed the output into both tracks. Set the right manual level control for normal peaking. Set the left manual level control 15dB lower, so loud sounds will not totally over-modulate. That way, you are protected from severe audio distortion without having to rely on automatic level control.

Recording Audio Separately

The sure way to infallible audio is simultaneous recording on a separate DAT machine, with a simultaneous feed directly into the camcorder.

No matter how ambidextrous the camera operator, it is, nevertheless, counter-productive for one person to be expected to execute graceful pans and tilts, with elegant zooms and follow-focus, while carefully keeping the frame perfectly composed, consistent in continuity, properly lit, appropriately white-balanced—all the while monitoring audio and adjusting levels to avoid over modulation or excessive ambience.

Having a separate sound system provides not only an extra set of ears, and hands, but it also serves as a backup system that protects the original tape. This can be especially helpful when the final project is going to be mixed in a studio. Handing over the DAT is much simpler, and safer, than giving up the cassette holding all the original pictures.

Many documentary and news crews employ an audio person to handle the microphone and mix the audio. The sound is fed into a mixer, whose knobs control audio input levels. The signal is then passed along to a wireless transmitter, which sends it to the camcorder, where it is picked up by a wireless receiver attached to the back. The audio is then fed to the XLR audio inputs, and recorded on tape.

In either situation, the audio can be split onto separate tracks. You can put a lavalier output on the right channel, and a shotgun mic for ambience on the left channel. Popular mikes are Sennheiser's ME66 and ME67 shotgun modules for the K6 battery/phantom power unit, and Sony's ECM-77B and ECM-44B lavalier.

For dramatic productions, using an electronic slate jam-synced to the timecoded DAT will save lots of agony in the editing room, even if it takes a few seconds more on set. You can identify scene and take number, but more importantly, have a "head sticks" synchronization point to enable laying in audio over the reference track of the camcorder.

Wireless microphone receivers like Sony's WRR-855B can be attached to DSR DVCAM camcorders with a CA-WR855 camera adapter.

Lenses

Comparison of CCD Size and Film Apertures

The chart at right is a life-size drawing showing the relative sizes of different CCDs and how they compare with the image area on 16mm and 35mm film.

CCDs are measured diagonally. So a 1/2" chip is measured along opposite corners. The aspect ratio is 4:3, which is the same as a 1.33:1 film gate.

Notice how 16mm and the 1/2" CCD are the same.

The amazing thing is how small a 1/4" CCD really is.

In case you're wondering, 16mm and 35mm are measurements of the width of the film, including sprocket area.

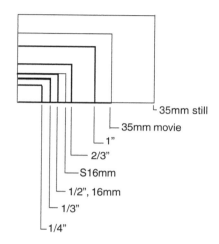

35mm still
35mm movie
1"
2/3"
S16mm
1/2", 16mm
1/3"
1/4"

Here, on the right, is a sample of 16mm film, which is indeed 16mm wide. The picture area in this case is composed in the Super16mm format, which is 1.66:1 (not quite the 16:9 of the video world, which can also be expressed as 1.77:1.)

You can't take an off-the-shelf motion picture lens and attach it to a camcorder. The back-focus is different. Back-focus is the distance required from the lens mount to the chip, and in a film camera, from the lens mount to the film itself. Three-chip camcorders add their own limitations because of the beam splitters, so manufacturers have specific lines of video lenses.

Back focus and collimation

A lens for still or motion picture cameras has to be designed so all frequencies of light focus onto a single plane, which is the film itself. Since red, blue and green light travels at different wavelengths, the lens must compensate. A 3-chip DVCAM camcorder separates the three colors with a beamsplitter, so video lenses are designed with that in mind. You cannot simply mount a still or film lens onto a 3-chip DVCAM camcorder without modification. Similarly, to mount a video lens onto a film camera, you must add an additional element that combines and re-focuses the three colors.

A word on back focus. Most interchangeable video lenses have a back focus adjustment to adjust the flange to prism distance. According to several lens technicians, this is a vestige from the era when tubes were used in cameras, and adjustment constantly had to be tweaked. Ideally, once the lens is set, its back focus should not have to be readjusted, because the mounts in DVCAM camcorders are robust and well-protected. Furthermore, a collimator is more accurate than eye-focusing on a chart.

In the field, you can quickly check your lens. Set up the camcorder on a tripod 6 feet (2m) from a Siemens Star focus chart. Zoom in all the way. Adjust focus. Now, zoom out to full wide. The chart should remain sharp. If not, take your DSR-PD100A, PD150 or 250 camcorder in for service, since back focus is not a user option. Back focus on lenses that mount on the DSR-300A and DSR-500WS can be adjusted by loosening the back focus screw and turning the lens ring until the image is sharpest at wide angle.

Lens Specs

When you see specifications for DVCAM lenses, you'll see something like this: 4.2-42mm f1.8-2.8

This is a 10x (10 times) zoom. If you divide the telephoto end (42mm) by the wide end (4.2mm), you get 10. The letter "f" is the maximum f-stop of the lens (wide open).

In this case, the most you can open the iris is f1.8. The second f-stop, 2.8, shows that the optical designers of this lens "cheated" to make it smaller and lighter. To keep the amount of light passing through the lens the same at both wide angle and telephoto, they would have had to make the glass elements much larger. So, the f2.8 means that's the maximum aperture when you zoom in to 42mm. It also means that if you zoom all the way from wide to tight continuously during the shot, there will be a one-stop darkening of the image from beginning to end. Automatic exposure circuits will probably compensate, but remember this when in manual mode.

DVCAM Lenses and 35mm Equivalents

For those cinematographers with 35mm motion picture lens angles of view firmly committed to memory, volatile or otherwise, the quick and slightly inaccurate—but close enough—conversion is to multiply by 8 for a 1/4" CCD and multiply by 9 for a 1/3" CCD.

Lens Attachments

If you want to shoot wider or tighter than the lens that comes with the camcorder, you can purchase wide-angle and telephoto lens adapters. They screw into the front filter thread of the existing lens.

Doublers, or tele-extenders, do just that. They magnify the image two times. They typically come in strengths of 2x and 1.6x.

So, if your zoom lens is 4 to 10mm, the doubler makes it the equivalent of 8 to 20mm.

Wide angle attachments typically widen the field of view of the zoom lens. They typically come in .6x, .7x and .8x strenghs. You can purchase these adapters from the manufacturer, or from specialists like Century Precision Optics or Optex.

Century Precision and OpTex

Century Precision Optics (www.centuryoptics.com) and OpTex (www.optexint.com) have been making converters and adapters for motion picture lenses for years, and now have a complete line of accessories for DVCAM lenses.

Wide Angle Adapters

There are many wide angle adapters, including .3x, .5x, .6x, .7x and .8x. No exposure compensation is required. The .3x adapter is considered a fisheye lens, with a horizontal view angle of 130°. Be aware that some wide angle adapters limit zoom range because of vignetting at certain focal lengths.

Tele-Extenders

The 1.6x extender attaches to the front of your lens, and does not cause any light loss. The 2x extender is intended for removable lenses, and fits between the camera body and the lens. It "eats" two stops of light.

Diopters

Diopters work like reading glasses. They allow the lens to focus closer. Single element diopters typically come in strengths of +1/2, +1 and +2.

They are relatively inexpensive, but can cause a bit of chromatic aberration and softening of the image. Century's Achromatic Diopters use two elements and are optically much better, and of course, cost more. They come in strengths of +1.6, 2, 2.6, 3.5, 4 and 7.

Anamorphic

Anamorphic adapters can be helpful on native 4:3 chip camcorders with fixed lenses, like the DSR-PD100A, DSR-PD150 and DSR-250.

If you're planning on a theatrical release, an anamorphic adapter will provide a wide-screen aspect ratio by "squeezing" the image horizontally. This image is "unsqueezed" when projected or handled in post. Be careful with vignetting.

By recording in the 4:3 mode, you are taking advantage of all the pixels, rather than using

OpTex Anamorphic

the fewer horizontal lines (fewer pixels) on the camcorder's menu-set 16:9 format. Be careful with anamorphic adapters—there may be some vignetting around the edges at wide angle which you will not see in the viewfinder. Check the monitor.

Lenses for DSR-300A, 500WS

The DSR-500WS camcorder uses video lenses designated for 2/3" CCDs. This includes most existing lenses that fit Betacam SP, Digital Betacam and HD.

The DSR-300A uses 1/2" video lenses.

There's a wide, and ever-evolving selection of superb optics from both Canon and Fujinon. Refer to their web sites, at:

www.usa.canon.com/indtech/broadcasteq/bctv/

and www.fujinonbroadcast.com

How do we decide which lens to rent or buy? We consider zoom range— what the focal length is at its widest and tightest ends. How fast is the lens: what is its maximum aperture? We wants smooth zooms, both electric and manual, along with smooth focus. Try the lens on the intended camcorder, either at a dealer, trade show or rental house.

By the way, zoom lenses are often calibrated in T Stops, which takes into account the light lost after traveling through many optical elements. F Stops are basically the same thing, without calculation of light loss.

The following charts show some of the characteristic lens specifications.

Fujinon 1/2" and 2/3" Lenses

	S15x6.1 EVM/ ERD	S10x3.5 EVM/ ERD	S12x5 RM
FOCAL LENGTH	(1x)6.1-91.5mm (2x)12.2-183mm	(1x)3.5-35mm (2x)7-70mm	5-60mm
ZOOM RATIO	15x	10x	12x
EXTENDER	2x	2x	NO
Maximum Relative Aperture	1:1.4(6.1-82mm) 1:1.6(91.5mm)	1:1.4(3.5-29mm) 1:1.7(35mm)	1:1.8(5-54mm) 1:2.0(60mm)
Minimum Object Distance (M.O.D.)	0.65m	0.3m	0.5m
Object Dimensions at M.O.D.	6.1mm 639x479mm 91.5mm 43x32mm	3.5mm 618x464mm 35mm 62x46mm	5mm 638x478mm 60mm 53x39mm
MACRO	YES	YES	YES
FILTER THREAD	M82x0.75	M127x0.75	M82x0.75
LENGTH	210.3mm	249mm	183mm
WEIGHT (w/out lens hood)	1.4kg/1.5kg	1.85kg/1.92kg	1.2kg

Canon 1/2" and 2/3" Lenses

18x	18x with built-in doubler
9-162mm f1.8/2.5 18x zoom, internal focus YJ18x9B KRS (for 2/3")	9-162mm f1.8/2.5 18x zoom 18-324mm f3.6/5 with internal 2x YJ18x9B IRS (for 2/3")
6.7-121mm f1.4/1.8 18x zoom, internal focus YH18x6.7 KRS (for 1/2")	6.7-121mm f1.4/1.8 18x zoom 13.4-242mm f2.8/3.7 with internal 2x YH18x6.7 IRS (for 1/2")

Fujinon 1/2" and 2/3" Lenses

	S17x6.6 RM	S19x6.5 RM/ERM*	S22x5.8 EVM/ ERD*
FOCAL LENGTH	6.6-112mm	6.5-123mm (1x)6.5-123mm* (2x13-246mm*	(1x)5.8-128mm (2x)11.6-256mm
ZOOM RATIO	17x	19x	22x
EXTENDER	NO	NO 2x*	2x
Maximum Relative Aperture	1:1.4(6.6-90mm) 1:1.9(112mm)	1:1.4(6.5-91mm) 1:1.9(123mm)	1:1.4(5.8-94mm) 1:1.9(128mm)
Minimum Object Distance (M.O.D.)	0.9m	0.9m	0.8m
Object Dimensions at M.O.D.	6.6mm 808x606mm 112mm 48x36mm	6.5mm 835x626mm 123mm 44x33mm	5.8mm 823x617mm 128mm 37x28mm
MACRO	YES	YES	YES
FILTER THREAD	M82x0.75	M82x0.75	M95x1
LENGTH	181.8mm	204.1mm	219.4mm
WEIGHT (w/out lens hood)	1.25kg	1.35kg 1.45kg*	1.7kg 1.77kg*

Canon 1/2" and 2/3" Lenses

12x	12x with built-in doubler
6.5-78mm f2/2.6 12x zoom, internal focus YJ12x6.5B KRS (for 2/3")	6.5-78mm f2/2.6 12x zoom 13-156mm f4/5.2 with internal 2x YJ12x6.5B IRS (for 2/3")
4.8-58mm f1.5/2 12x zoom, internal focus YH12x4.8KRS (for1/2")	4.8-58mm f 1.5/2 9.6-116mm f 3/4 with internal 2x YH12x4.8 IRS (for 1/2")

Matteboxes and Filters

A mattebox keeps flares off your lens, and has trays to hold filters. Flares are caused when the sun or artificial lights shine onto your lens. They're pretty, but you may not want them covering the face of the governor giving a press conference. Sunshades usually come with the camcorder, but you have to buy the mattebox as an aftermarket accessory.

Most of the sunshades that come with camcorders do not provide for filters. That leaves you with several choices.

The simplest are round, screw-in filters. They come in as many sizes as there are thread diameters for cameras. This doubtlessly provides eternal employment for the manufacturers of filters, because whenever you use a different camera or lens, you need a different filter. You can purchase step-up or step-down adapter rings. Or you can buy square filters that fit into a filter tray that slides into the mattebox.

For documentaries, news and events, lightweight clamp-on matteboxes and filter-holder/sunshade combinations are available. Some of the best come from Chrosziel, Birns and Sawyer, and CineTech.

Chrosziel Mattebox

Studio and dramatic work suggests a mattebox that slides onto rods that attach below the camcorder. You can also add a follow focus assembly for keeping the action critically sharp. Chrosziel makes excellent matteboxes and follow focus units. Formatt matteboxes (distributed by Ste-Man Inc) are also good. A French Flag with flex arm can help keep light off the finder or lens.

Some Filter Sizes

Camcorder	Filter Size
DSR-PD100A	52mm
DSR-PD150, DSR-250	58mm
DSR-500WS w/ Canon YJ18x9; A17x9 RM Fujinon DSR-300A w/ Canon YH18x6.7; S17x6.6 RM Fujinon	82mm

Filters

Be selective and use them tastefully. Tiffen Pro-Mists come in strengths of 1/8 to 3, and can add an elegant, painterly quality—but I would rarely recommend using any grade higher than 1/8 or 1/4 on DVCAM. SoftFX filters soften facial blemishes, and are a kind of optical equivalent of Sony's Skin Detail function. There are glass and plastic filters on the market. Use glass. Plastic, even durable lexan, can distort the image at long focal lengths.

Regular, or white, Pro-Mist filters "smooth" out textures, and add a slight glow to highlights, remove harsh edges, slightly reduce contrast and provide a more "film" look to video.

Black Pro Mist filters are similar, with slightly less flare in highlights than white Pro-Mists. Contrast is reduced slightly by lightening shadows and darkening highlights.

Soft Contrast filters darkening highlights while allowing shadow areas to stay dark, producing a softer, less intense color.

Soft/FX filters have tiny lenslets embedded in the glass. They retain overall image clarity for portraits, softening unwanted details like wrinkles and skin blemishes, while the eyes remain sharp.

Ultra Contrast filters lower contrast by lightening shadow areas without causing any flare or halo effects from direct bright light sources, reflections or highlights. They use ambient light to lower contrast evenly.

Fog Filters give the effect of a natural fog by causing lights to flare and "fog" to appear where none previously existed.

Enhancing Filters are made of didymium glass to create warm vibrant colors by selectively improving saturation of reds and oranges.

Graduated Filters usually have a neutral density gray or a color in the top half, and are clear in the bottom half. The transition between the two is made either Hard (for telephoto shots) or Soft (for wider angles). ND Grads help to tone down bright skies. Blue Color, Sunset and Straw Grads can make a hazy sky look beautiful.

Blenders are like grads, but do not have a definitive line between clear and color, making the transition gradually over the entire horizontal surface of the filter.

Set Camcorder to Manual Control

When using filters, be sure to turn off auto-pilot control of the camcorder. With automatic white-balance and exposure turned on, the camcorder will try to overcome the effects of the filter.

Lighting

Film students and producers, perhaps united by their common bond of eternal optimism or bottom line, often ask whether digital video still requires lighting. Like all things photographic, if it doesn't look good by eye, shooting it on digital viedo is not going to rescue your career.

The best way to learn about lighting is to go to the movies and try to figure out how they did the lighting. Study great paintings, and then pretend you have to light the same scene. How would you do it? Visit museums to see paintings in their intended colors. Visit museums on the web. Among the many excellent sites:

Metropolitan Museum NY is at: www.metmuseum.org

The National Gallery in Washingon, DC: www.nga.gov

The Tate Museum, London: www.tate.org.uk

The Louvre, Paris: www.louvre.fr

Musée D'Orsay, Paris: www.musee-orsay.fr

ARt Museum Network: www.amn.org

Web Museum, Paris: www.ibiblio.org/wm/

There are many more. Search them at www.google.com.

Beware easily portable lighting kits and on-board sunguns. They can be wonderful tools or terrible traps, ensnaring the unwitting in a downward spiral of poor technique. Because the lights themselves are small, harsh shadows can result if the lights are used unmodified.

Remember: the larger the source, the softer and more natural the shadows. So, bouncing the light from these small fixtures into large reflective surfaces will soften the light and its accompanying shadows. Use bed sheets, muslins, foamcore, or even the wall. Large sheets of diffusion material, similar to shower curtain, but fire-resistant, help soften light when bouncing is impractical.

When shooting on location, we usually try to place our lights outside, and aim them through the windows of the room. Using large 12,000 to 18,000 watt HMI lights softened slightly with Lee 216 or Rosco Opal Tough Frost creates a beautiful, single source natural look. A standard location package will usually include a generator and a ten-ton truck to carry all the lights, along with lots of grip equipment to control them, because beautiful lighting is mostly about taking light away, selectively, from certain areas.

Lighting kits large and small are made by Lowel, Ianiro, Mole, LTM, Desisti and ARRI. Remember, the more equipment you have, the larger the vehicle needed to transport it. Keep it simple and small. Kinoflos are cool, soft fluorescents. Your favorite expendable supply store should provide 4' x 8' Foamcore and Beadboard. Chimera Lightbanks, metallic umbrellas, Flexfills and Litepanels are some of the many commercially available products used in the never-ending quest to shape and control light.

You don't have to spend a fortune on lighting equipment. The credits on your next low-budget opus can read "Grip and Lighting Equipment supplied by Home Depot." Construction work lights cost less than a hundred dollars, and come complete with stands, halogen bulbs and cable. Fluorescent light banks can be improvised from twenty-dollar shop fixtures. "Rags" can be made from bed sheets and shower curtains. Your large diffusion material can be 4'x6' frosted nylon shower curtains for $14 each.

Twin 1K Tungsten Halogen work lights, complete with stands, cost around $58 each. With a DVCAM's manual white balance, you don't have to worry that the bulbs will not be exactly 3200 K. Set up the lights, hold up a white card in front of the key light, and set your white balance.

Hopefully, your opus lit by Ace Hardware will be so successful that your next epic has a normal budget, and you'll wonder how you ever got by without a well-outfitted professional 5 or 10 ton grip and electric trucks.

One of my mentors was Director of Photography and founder of Lowel-Light, Ross Lowell. I met him when I worked on staff at a production company that owned a lot of Lowel-Lights. At the time, they came with clever chains to remotely spot and flood the bulbs. However, whenever we went out on a job, the gaffers and electricians snipped the chains off, because they either felt the chains got in the way or that a ladder was a better way to spot and flood the light. I thought the chains were a good idea, and made almost monthly trips to Ross' offices on West 54th Street to have them replaced. One day, Ross showed me a large shipment from someone in England. The lights belonged to Stanley Kubrick, and he also wanted his missing chains replaced. It appeared that Stanley Kubrick, Ross and I were the only people in the world who liked them, because later versions, now called the "DP" light, come chain-less. All of this is by way of recommending Ross Lowell's excellent book on lighting, *Matters of Light and Depth*.

Tripods and Heads

The tripod and head are perhaps the most essential camcorder accessories. A fluid head adds elegance to moves and stabilizes telephoto shots. The operator can pan, tilt and zoom (assuming the zoom control is attached to the pan handle) with one hand, leaving the other hand free to operate a Dutch head, tweak focus, grab a cell phone or a cup of coffee. Viscous fluid in the head, usually silicone, smooths your pans and tilts. Mechanical heads look, well, mechanical.

head

tripod

spreader

Most tripods have three pointed tips at the bottom of each leg assure a firm grip on soft ground as well as the certain wrath of the homeowner whose wooden floor you have just scratched and perforated.

A spreader protects precious floors, and also prevents the embarrassment of watching the camcorder tumble onto the slippery marble as the legs slip apart. Some spreaders mount halfway up the leg. These require separate "feet" to cover the tips. Some tripods use rubber bushings, threaded onto the tips, that retract when needed.

There are two mounting options on top of the tripod: flat or ball. A ball receptacle makes leveling the camcorder much easier than individually adjusting the legs. There are three common sizes of ball receptacles for tripods: 75mm, 100mm and 150mm diameter. For DVCAM, 75mm is the most popular. Carbon fiber tripods are about a pound lighter than aluminum, and a two-section tripod will extend from about 16 to 60 inches.

Low angle shots are accomplished with "baby legs" and "high hats." Some tripods can be configured so the legs spread out flat on the floor, thus doing double duty.

Baseplates

There are many ways to attach the camcorder to a tripod head: direct bolt or quick release plate. Each manufacturer has its own size and style, along with its own method of balancing the camcorder on top.

Miller Quick-Release Plate

Mounting

DSR-PD100A, DSR-PD150

The DSR-PD100A and DSR-PD150 camcorders have 1/4"x20 threads at the bottom of the camcorder. Most quick release (also called touch-and-go) plates come with 1/4"x20 and 3/8"x16 captive bolts. Use the 1/4"x20 — but be careful because the socket is rather shallow.

Do not force the tripod mounting bolt too deep. If the bolt is too long, it could crack the housing and damage electronic parts inside.

DSR-250, 300a, 500WA

The DSR-250, DSR-300A and DSR-500WS require a VCT-U14 Tripod Adaptor. It comes with the latter two, but must be ordered separately with the DSR-250.

Screw the tripod head's quick release plate into the bottom of the VCT-U14 Adaptor.

Be sure the safety pin is cocked. If not, move the release lever forward. To mount the camcorder, slide it forward into the dovetail until you hear it click into place.

Heads

Very few camera operators will agree on what defines a perfect head. Some operators prefer a stiff feel; I like a loose touch. Some like thick handles, other like thin.

The big names in fluid heads and tripods are Sachtler, Cartoni, Miller, Gitzo, Vinten, Manfrotto and O'Connor.

Most heads have a safety latch to prevent accidental release. Pull down on the safety latch, and slide the release to the left to unlock the camcorder. When mounting the camcorder, always double check that it is securely latched by pulling up on the camcorder itself.

The sliding top balance plate compensates for camcorders

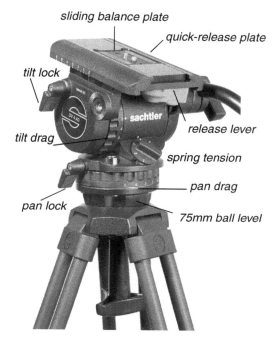

sliding balance plate

quick-release plate

tilt lock

release lever

tilt drag

spring tension

pan drag

pan lock

75mm ball level

that are front or back heavy. To balance your camcorder, release the pan and tilt locks. Turn the friction dials to 0. Move the balance plate until the camcorder is level. Then, set the spring tension to counter-balance the weight of the camcorder, and turn the tension dials to a comfortable level.

It's ironic that professional tripods and heads can cost almost as much as the camcorder itself. Fortunately, a new line of cheaper digital video support systems are appearing. Unfortunately for your back, it is usually true that heavier tripods and heads offer more stability and smoother moves.

The main thing is to choose a tripod that isn't a burden to take with you wherever you go. If you're shooting news or documentaries or sports, it should be small and light enough to fit in or on a backpack.

Soft, nylon tripod cases are much easier to handle than rigid tubes. However, if you're going to ship the tripod and head by air, be sure to pack your soft case inside a hard one. Carbon fiber and aluminum legs will not survive an unprotected trip beneath a load of Samsonite suitcases.

The best way to choose a head and tripod is to check it out with the intended camcorder at a trade show or your favorite dealer.

I recommend a head that tilts straight up and straight down. Most of the Vinten digital video heads do; Sachtler, Miller, Cartoni and the others come pretty close.

For the DSR-PD100A and DSR-PD150, Sachtler's DV4 with carbon fiber legs is one of the good choices. The Sachtler DV12, shown at right, is well-balanced for the DSR-250, 300A or 500WS. Shooters who need to tower above the crowd will appreciate the center-post pneumatic column of the Hot Pod, which extends the shooting position to over 78" (2m). Tripod and head weigh about 16 pounds.

If you don't have to constantly jostle the paparazzi for an unobstructed, high-angle view, you can save money and about 5 pounds of weight with double-stage carbon fiber legs. Aluminum legs are considerably cheaper than carbon fibre, not much heavier, and almost as durable.

For expedition and really remote work with a DSR-PD100A, the Gitzo Mountaineer Compact G1128 is a 4-section carbon fiber tripod, 19 inches long when folded, that weighs a mere 2½ pounds. It has a flat top.

The DSR-PD150 may be happier on one of three other Gitzo carbon fiber tripods, called Mountaineer Mk2, that range from 4.5 to 6.75 pounds and can be configured with 75mm or 100mm bowls on top for quick leveling. Aluminum legs cost a few hundred dollars less, but weigh about 1.5 pounds more.

Other interesting choices for the DSR-PD100A and 150 are Gitzo's 3-pound G2380 head, and Manfrotto's 501 Video Head with 3221 Video Tripod.

Miller's Sprinter Tripod (distributed by Ste-Man in the US) simplifies the process of adjusting a two-stage tripod with lever locks positioned next to each other. Multiple stage tripods collapse to smaller sizes, but previously took longer to set up.

Remote Control

When using a fluid head, it is essential to have external control of your zooms. Trying to wrap your right hand around the handgrip with a tripod handle poking you in the stomach is both painful and difficult. Tripod handle controls are available from Sony along with aftermarket ones from VariZoom, Libec, Canon and Fujinon.

Camcorder Care

The DVCAM camcorders do not require lubrication. You should not use grease anywhere. Try to keep them out of dusty, moist or salt air as much as possible. Use rain covers, plastic bags or garbage bags in these "hostile" environments.

Around salt water and humid areas, wipe the external surfaces of the camcorder with CRC 5-56 or LPS 1 (not LPS 3). These rust-inhibiting formulations are not greasy or slippery (WD-40 is). Use a cotton rag on large surfaces. Use a foam swab, Kimwipe or lens tissue for screw heads and hard-to-get places. Use a small amount—a little goes a long way. Apply to the rag first. Do NOT spray the camcorder. Do not wipe or spray inside the tape transport area, or around the glass lens elements. Do not use on the battery or on electrical connections. Here, you will need an electrical contact restorer, such as CONTACT RE-NU or CRC 2-26.

Most camcorders will run from 32° Fahrenheit to +110° Fahrenheit, and most will do better than that. In very hot climates—desert, sand, tropics— put a Space Blanket, white barney or T-shirt on the camcorder to reflect the sun's heat.

In very cold conditions, a black cloth or black side of a space blanket will absorb sunlight. A heater barney made of neoprene or foam will extend the temperature range. When it's really cold, stuff a Grabber MyCoal handwarmer inside (www.grabberwarmers.com). Wearing a battery belt or battery vest under your parka will extend run life. An electric sock, popular with ice fishermen and skiers, will also work to heat the camcorder's on-board battery.

Zoom lenses can become excessively stiff in Arctic-cold conditions. You may want to have them winterized by an authorized service shop, where the grease is removed and replaced by a lighter lubricant.

In very sticky, humid conditions, the tape can stick to the head when it is stopped. Try not to keep the camcorder in pause for long periods, and eject tapes at the end of the day. NEVER lubricate this area with anything other than head cleaner.

Head Cleaning

Remember that DVCAM tapes have a lubricant layer that helps prevent build-up on the heads. Under normal conditions, you should not have to clean the heads often. When working in dusty, salty or other "hostile" environments, use a Sony Head Cleaning Cassette when needed to clean the heads of your camcorder or VTR. The DV-12CLD is for standard (large) cassettes; DVM-12CLD is for Mini cassettes. Store these cleaning cassettes in a Ziploc plastic bag in between use.

Lens Cleaning

There is really only one good way to clean a dusty lens or optical surface. Blow plain air with a hand operated air syringe. (Dust-Off is more convenient, but will leave a chemical residue which smears.)

If the dust is gritty, gently brush it off with a fine camel's hair brush which you have reserved for lens use only.

If the lens has been smudged with fingerprints, or smeared, dirty or splattered with salt water spray, squirt one or two drops of lens fluid (Pancro is recommended) on a crumpled lens tissue. Wipe the tissue in a circular motion. Dry the lens immediately with a dry piece of lens tissue. Also wipe in a circular motion—but don't scrub. If the lens is really dirty, you will have to repeat this process a number of times until the residue disappears.

Never use a dry lens tissue, because it may scratch the lens. Lens tissues, like the paper on this page, are just trees that have been ground up. Do you want to scratch your lens with the branch of a tree?

Microfiber cloths like Luminex are also excellent for cleaning lenses. But they should not be used to scrub away stubborn smears instead of lens fluid. Also, the microfiber cloths should be washed often. Drying the lens with a clean, photographic microfiber cloth is probably even better than using paper lens tissue.

Eyepiece and Eyecup

When the rubber eyecup becomes encrusted with donut goo, buy a box of Isopropyl Alcohol Swabs from your local drugstore. The swabs come in handy foil packets.

Clean the eyepiece lens with a microfiber cloth. Don't use Isopropyl swabs, lens cleaners or solvents on the eyepiece. Some of the elements are plastic, and may be damaged or smeared.

LCD Viewing Screen

Try not to touch the plastic LCD screen. It inevitably becomes smudged, and you can clean it off with a dry microfiber optical cloth. Do not use alcohol, solvents or lens fluid.

Stiffened nylon and velcro monitor hoods are very useful for keeping glare off the screen in bright sunlight. The original ones were made by Hoodman, which still offers the most choices of size and shape. Other models, by several companies, abound.

Low-Tech Rain Covers

Perhaps in response to the observation that most crews are better protected in their penultimate Patagonia high-tech, multi-colored, breathable, waterproof, windproof, windowed, toggled, tabbed and Velcro-vented raingear than their camcorders, several well-designed rain covers have emerged from rental houses, from Camera Essentials in Hollywood, Ewa-Marine in Germany, and Scubacam in London.

After it rains, don't forget to dry the covers out. Mildew is not a pleasant odor.

If you need a disposable cover, there is a clear, cheap, garbage-bag rain cover. Having scoured the janitorial supply catalogs of the world, I recommend Extra Heavy Duty 4 mil Clear Chiswick Poly Bags, which are sold in lots of a thousand. They are available in a multitude of sizes costing less than a dollar a bag. Cut a hole for the lens, and attach the bag over the mattebox with a Velcro strap.

Cut another hole for the eyepiece, and use a rubber band to hold it in place. Bunch up the unused part of the bag with a clip. Of course, you can always use a lowly, ordinary garbage bag. But Chiswick's clear alternative lets you see what is inside, and for a modest extra fee, they will add your name or logo.

High-Tech Rain Covers

The one rule of rain covers is that one cover will rarely be acceptable for all configurations of a camcorder: handheld, on tripod, on a car mount, underslung on a remote head. You will very often need several variations.

Scubacam and Ewa-Marine DVCAM rain covers are higher-tech than the garbage bags we usually use, and easier to use. A provision in the design gives the operator fully unhindered viewing of an on-board monitor, while still being able to use the conventional viewfinder.

Ewa-Marine rain covers have an optical glass port to cover the front element of the lens. The cover is made of PVC that remains flexible from 14° to 158° F.

On the Scubacam covers, the viewfinder is secured by a drawstring that pulls tightly over the viewfinder eyecup. An adjustable lens strap holds the cover over the lens hood of the camcorder. A clear viewing panel is located over the main body of the camcorder to enable the operator to see the camcorder functions. A two inch elongated tube behind the video door allows the operator to access the lens for focus control.

Rain covers from Camera Essentials are clear plastic.

Sun/Dust Covers

A camcorder can get as hot as the interior of your car on a scorching, summer day, which, if you read the small print on most video cassettes, the manufacturer warns against. Don't leave the camcorder inside your trunk or hot vehicle. Scubacam and Camera Essentials have a line of sun and dust covers made of silver, reflective 4 oz. nylon. Space blankets or old, white T-shirts, clipped together with plastic spring clips, will work in a pinch.

Splash Bags

Scubacam makes a splash (repeat: Splash) housing of 1/8" (2.5mm) natural yellow latex, which is advertised to be waterproof to 22' (7 meters) when sealed with its heavy duty watertight zipper. It can be handheld or mounted on a tripod. A 30' long umbilical cord contains two power cables, remote on/off and video cables which attach to the camcorder with waterproof external connectors.

The Scubacam mini DVCAM housing can be submerged to a maximum depth of 7 meters. Do not leave the unit unattended at any time while underwater.

Caution: Before every use, carry out a visual inspection to determine if there is any damage to the housing. To check, seal the unit without the camcorder inside, and submerge it in water, remove and inspect for leaks.

There are also Scubacam models for larger shoulder-resting DSR-250, 300A and 500WS.

Ewa-Marine makes a similar splash housing. The advertised depth is 5 meters (about 15 feet). Again, I would suggest the emphasis is more on splash, and less on underwater.

Underwater Housings

For serious protection of your investment underwater, your DVCAM camcorder should be used inside a rigid underwater housing. Some of the respected names in the field are:

Amphibico (www.amphibico.com)
Seacam (www.seacamsys.com)
Gates (www.gateshousings.com)
Ikelite (www.ikelite.com)
Oceanimages (www.oceanimagesinc.com)

Cases and Shipping

It is best, though not always practical, to hand-carry the camcorder with you wherever you go. Not only will you avoid the wear and tear of shipping, but you'll also avoid the sinking feeling of being the only person left at baggage claim still watching an empty conveyor belt. But be aware that airlines may refuse to let you carry the camcorder on board. So, take the empty camcorder body case with you.

Soft-sided shoulder bags and backpacks that fit under airline seats are great. A large, padded shoulder bag with adjustable foam-lined compartments can carry the camcorder, accessory lenses, filters, batteries, charger and tape. Having these items with you all saves time and footwork. Tenba, Lowe, KATA, Portabrace, Tamrac and Tough Traveler are popular brands of camcorder shoulder bags.

If your style is more corporate, you'll be happy with attaché size waterproof cases by Pelican #1550 (19" x 14" x 7.75"), Pelican 1450 (15" x 10.5" x 6"), Tundra SK821 (20.9" x 12.9" x 8.4"), or Tundra SK518 (17.8" x 12.8" x 5.1"). Aluminum Halliburton cases look great until you ding them the first time. Furthermore, they are not waterproof.

Monitors, lenses and fragile accessories should be shipped in cases with generous padding to protect the equipment from the rigors of airline handling and dropping from cargo hold to runway. Thermodyne ABS Cases, which are waterproof, lightweight and resilient, come in many sizes, including a popular configuration of 24" x 18" x 14".

Fiberglass-covered plywood cases made by A&J and Calzone are heavier, not waterproof, but more durable. "Rigidised" aluminum cases are lighter and popular in Europe, since they only seem to be made in England and are never spelled with a "z".

It's a good idea to have three inches of foam surrounding all pieces of equipment.

Expeditions

Lowe makes good expedition packs for far-off places. For ski and mountaineering shoots, smaller day packs with padded compartments are helpful. For extreme conditions, you can substitute clothing and expedition gear for the foam.

To get to location, you can ship the equipment in the packs. The packs should, however, be protected by a rigid case. A waterproof Thermodyne will protect the pack from crushing and flooding. And you never know, you might be able to use the Thermodyne as a life raft.

Tripod Case

I don't like round tripod cases. They roll around and waste space. Most lightweight tripod systems will fit in one TEK Series Rolling Tripod Case from Tamrac. It is a foam padded "soft case," and has a couple of skateboard wheels. Nalpak and A&J make good octagonal cases.

Cutting Cases

The most important accessory of all are the cases in which you pack, coddle, ship and protect your investment. Soft-sided shoulder bags, backpacks and wheeled soft-sided cases are best for local work where the equipment is carried by people, cars or vans. My favorite soft-sided bags come from Lowe, PortaBrace, Tenba, Kata, Tamrac and Lightware. For serious expeditions and hostile environments, LowePro makes back packs, along with the Vidcam series of shoulder bags and the Omni /Extreme series of soft bags that fit inside waterproof shells for shipping.

Once you get into air travel and shipping, you need durable, water-resistant ATA style cases from Pelican or Thermodyne. A good source is Nalpak, which also supplies tripod cases and Magliner carts to wheel all the stuff around.

To cut out the foam inside these cases, an electric knife left over from your Thanksgiving feast makes an excellent saw and is a lot easier to use than an X-Acto knife. Lubricate the blades with silicone from time to time. For hard-to-reach areas, use an X-Acto knife with a 2" blade (#26).

Use 2 inch thick foam for the first layer, then some 1 inch layers, then 1/4 inch, and finally 1/2 inch. Cut layer by layer, working your way down. Outline the equipment directly onto the foam with a marker. Don't bother using templates. Glue the layers together with Contact Cement or 3M Foam and Fabric Spray Adhesive #74 for soft foams, and Barge Cement for hard foams. For custom foam jobs, go to A&J in Los Angeles, makers of durable custom cases and wonderful custom foam cut-outs.

Taping Cases

To protect the latches and ensure cases stay shut, always run some gaffers tape over the latches and over the two halves of the case.

Mark the destination address on the tape in case the equipment is lost.

It also helps to write down the flight number and destination airport should the airline tag be ripped off.

Gaffers tape now comes in numerous colors for easy identification.

VTRs

Using the camcorder to play back or edit tapes might save money, but it can shorten the life of the camera. If you plan to do a lot of editing, a professional deck with i.LINK, timecode and RS-422 serial control provides more accurate tape transport, better quality and faster shuttling.

A DVCAM VTR (or camcorder) can play back a tape recorded on DV and DVCAM. But, you can't play back a tape recorded in DVCAM format on a DV camera or deck. High-end DVCAM VTRs also play back DVCPRO tapes.

Probably the least expensive DVCAM/Mini DV Recorder/Player with RS-422 control is the Sony DSR-40, at a list price of $5,100.

Decks provide analog to digital converters. If you want a stand-alone A to D box, look at Sony's DVMC-DA2, as well as other brands.

DSR-11

Sony's DSR-11 is a low cost NTSC and PAL deck. It will not, however convert one format to the other. It accepts both Mini and Standard size cassettes, DV and DVCAM.

It has an i.LINK connector, and is one of the least expensive DVCAM VTRs to integrate into an IEEE 1394 nonlinear editing system. Note that it does not have an RS-422 connection, which you don't really need for input into XPress DV or FCP. List: $2,600.

DSR-20

The compact DSR-20 DVCAM Digital Videotape Recorder provides a wide range of video professionals with superior sound and image quality. Event and wedding videographers, multimedia creators and filmmakers also appreciate the convenience of its recording, playback and simple editing functions. The DSR-20 offers

three remote control interfaces, including LANC, Control S and RS-232C, as well as i.LINK (DV I/O based on IEEE-1394). This front-loading VTR accepts both Standard and Mini size cassettes, is easy to operate and offers versatile playback and recording capabilities. List price $3,950.

DSR-30

The DSR-30 has i.LINK, composite and S-Video connectors, and a jog/shuttle dial, making it a low-cost VTR to use with nonlinear editing systems. It's one of the few VTRs that can let you choose video output from a menu for either anamorphic (squeezed) or letterbox picture.

The DSR-30 accepts both Mini and Standard DVCAM/DV cassettes without adapters. List price $4,475.

DSR-40

The DSR-40 DVCAM VTR is half rack size, meaning it's about 8 3/8" wide. It has i.LINK DV In/Out for digital dubbing, editing and connection to IEEE-1394 video capture boards on desktop computers. An RS-422A remote control interfaces provides deck control from a nonlinear editing system such as Avid Media Composer or linear edit-controllers. Analog component and XLR audio outputs are available.

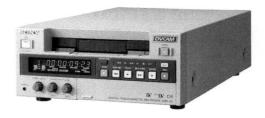

The DSR-40 accepts both Standard and Mini size cassettes.

A Dub button on the front panel expedites dubbing of the original tape and its time code when connected to another VTR or camcorder with the i.LINK connection. List price is $5,100.

DSR-1500

The DSR-1500 has many of the same features as the high-end DSR-2000, in a half-rack 3U size. The DSR-1500 can play consumer DV tapes (SP mode only) and DVCPRO 25 in addition to DVCAM—Standard and Mini sizes—without adaptors or additional settings.

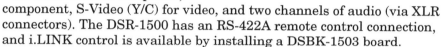

Standard analog output interfaces include: composite, component, S-Video (Y/C) for video, and two channels of audio (via XLR connectors). The DSR-1500 has an RS-422A remote control connection, and i.LINK control is available by installing a DSBK-1503 board.

The DSR-1500 can send ClipLink information data to a nonlinear editing system. It supports VITC Time Code, has a built-in signal generator for color bars or black burst, and 1 kHz tone or mute signal for audio.

Dimensions (WxHxD): 8 3/8" x 5 1/8" x 16 5/8". Weight: 13 lb. 3 oz. List price $5,695.

DSR-1600

The DSR-1600 has many of the features of the DSR-2000. It's a full-width deck with a jog/shuttle dial, jog audio, and slow motion playback. It has an RS-422A connection, and i.LINK is available by adding a DSBK-1803 board.

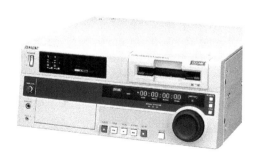

Analog and Digital connections include SDI for connection with Digital Betacam and Betacam SX, and SDTI (QSDI) interface.

With a Dynamic Motion Control editing controller, the DSR-1600 can vary playback speed from -0.5 to +0.5 times normal speed. The DSR-1600 supports ClipLink operation.

It has Process Control for analog and digital outputs— video level, chroma level, hue, Y/C delay Sync phase, SC phase and Set up (black) for composite, S-video, component and SDI outputs can be adjusted through the VTR menu or from an external TBC

remote controller. VITC time code is supported. The DSR-1600 has a built-in signal generator for color bars or black burst for video. List price is $6,650.

DSR-1800

The DSR-1800 also has many of the features of the DSR-2000. It features jog/shuttle control, jog audio, slow motion and editing functions. Optional analog and digital interfaces include SDI, SDTI (QSDI), and i. LINK/ IEEE-1394.

The Jog/Shuttle Dial provides variable speed playback at -0.5 to +0.5 times normal speed. The RS-422A connection is standard. An optional DSBK-1803 board is required for i.LINK control. ClipLink is supported, and Process Control

for analog and digital outputs is similar to the DSR-1500.

The DSR-1800 supports time code in the sub code area on a tape, and also VITC through all video signal interfaces. All four audio channels can be edited independently. Like the DSR-1500, the DSR-1800 has a built-in signal generator for color bars or black burst for video, and 1 kHz tone. List price $9,495.00.

DSR-2000

This is the top-of-the-line deck for DVCAM, for broadcast and high-end professional production. It includes a built-in edit control panel with jog/ shuttle dial and pre-read function. The DSR-2000 is the only model that plays back all DV25 tapes: consumer DV (both SP and LP recorded tapes), DVCPRO (25 Mbps) as well as DVCAM. The other models play back DV in SP mode only.

Double-Scan Playback can restore video and audio of misaligned tapes. The DSR-2000 also uses DMC for a wider digital slow playback range (-1.00 to +1.00) for noiseless slow-motion playback, jog audio, built-in video control (TBC), RS-422A interface, a built-in timecode generator and pre-read capability. It comes with analog component, S-Video, and composite video connectors, four balanced audio channels, SDI, SDTI (QSDI) and AES/EBU interfaces. With all of this, you might as well spring for the optional i.LINK/IEEE 1394 DV I/O interface board (DSBK-190), which is essential.

This is the first DVCAM VTR to offer pre-read editing capability, which allows the editor to make picture transitions with effects between two VTRs, as well as audio mixing and audio channel swapping with frame accuracy. The front panel, with its built-in Jog/Shuttle dial, allows two-machine editing. An optional front panel (DSBK-200) lets the editor control the functions of the VTR from 30 feet away. The DSR-2000 uses a direct reel and drum monitor mechanism for fast response. It has an industry-standard RS-422A Sony 9-pin remote control interface.

In summary, all conventional analog interfaces for video, audio and time code are supported by the DSR-2000. Its standard digital interfaces include: SDI, SDTI(QSDI), AES/EBU; i.LINK (DV In/Out), and SDTI (MPEG Out) are options.

The DSR-2000 supports ClipLink. List price $15,000.

DSR-85

The DSR85 is the first high-speed editing VTR that can transfer video and audio data at four times normal speed, through its SDTI (QSDI) interface. Intended for high-end broadcast and editing suites, it has full editing functions, including built-in TBC, TC generator/reader and RS-422A IF. List price $19,700.

Dockable Recorder/Player

DSR-1/1

The DSR-1/1 is the VTR section of a dockable camera system, in which the camera head and the recorder can be purchased separately. It replaces the DSR-1, which was the first dockable recorder for DVCAM format. The only difference between the two models is that the DSR-1/1 accepts BP-L series Lithium-Ion batteries.

The DSR-1/1 docks directly to a DXC (DXC-D30 or DXC-35D) digital or analog color camera. It features ClipLink operation, and when used with a DXC-D35, can use the camera set-up data file system, SetupNavi function, and freeze mix function. Its dual cassette mechanism accepts Standard and Mini sizes. There's a built-in time code generator/ reader and time stabilizer, record review function, back space

DXC-D35

editing, full color playback, DC output for wireless microphone, built-in external microphone power supply, and built-in self-diagnostics.

List price $8,075. Since this is like buying the engine without the car, you also need the camera. A DXC-D30 lists at $11,500 and a DXC-D35 is $12,155.

Portable DVCAM VTRs

DSR-V10 Video Walkman Recorder

Sony's smallest deck, DSR-V10, is useful for expeditions and remote documentaries. You can also use it on the airplane getting there to watch movies you've previously taped on DV or DVCAM.

The DSR-V10 has a 5.5" LCD monitor, weighs 2.2 pounds, and uses the same 7.2 volt batteries as the DSR-PD100A and DSR-PD150.

It has an i.LINK (DV IN/OUT) connector, and accepts Mini DV and Mini DVCAM cassettes.

There is no RS-422 deck control; however, there is a LANC connection.

List price $2,800.

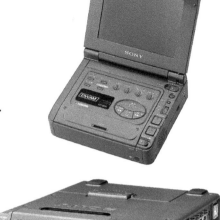

DSR-50 Portable Recorder

The DSR-50 is an 8 pound, AC or battery operated (BP-L90A/1) portable DVCAM VTR with a compact and lightweight design. It has a 2.5-inch diagonal built-in LCD monitor, so it's useful for location work. Features include 4-channel separate audio IN/OUT, timecode IN/OUT, 26-pin camera connector, and analog component OUT. The DSR-50 is useful as an ENG/EFP recorder or back-up recorder for news, documentary, or event videography, as well as a simple viewer or upload/download VTR

for nonlinear editing systems. List price $5,700.

DSR-70A Portable Editing Recorder

You might think of the DSR-70A as the ultimate Video Walkman and portable VTR—an all-in-one portable editing recorder with a 6.4 inch LCD monitor, speaker, jog/shuttle dial and linear edit controller keys. The DSR-70A is one of the high-end DVCAM Master Series VTRs, capable of playback of DV (SP), DVCAM and DVCPRO cassettes automatically without adapters or menu changes.

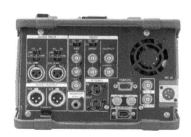

The DSR-70A can do full DVCAM editing, and when docked to the DNW-A25 Betacam SX Portable VTR, becomes a linear laptop editor, capable of VTR-to-VTR edits with DV, DVCAM, DVCPRO, Betacam SX and Betacam SP format tapes. It is used for ENG applications where video comes from multiple sources.

The DSR-70A has an SDI digital interface, for direct connection with Betacam SX VTRs and an RS-422 connection. The optional DSBK-160A provides both i.LINK/IEEE 1394 DV I/O and SDI input/output connections on a single board. List price $12,500.

Dubbing to Betacam SP UVW-1800

Sometimes I dub my DVCAM tapes to Betacam SP, using a Sony UVW-1800 videocassette recorder. Here are some pointers on how to avoid the dreaded black sync bar going across the picture.

1. Plug the S-Video connector into the S-Video Input on the back of the UVW-1800.

2. Plug the yellow video RCA jack into the VIDEO REF input connector on the UVW-1800 (you need an RCA to BNC adapter).

3. Be sure to set the VIDEO IN switch on the UVW-1800 front panel to S-VIDEO.

What we're doing is feeding S-Video into the UVW-1800. But we need a sync signal, and we're getting it from the composite video signal.

If you don't want to use S-Video, here's the same procedure for composite:

1. Plug the yellow video RCA jack into the VIDEO input connector on the UVW-1800.

2. Run a short BNC cable from the second BNC VIDEO input connector (it is essentially serving as an output) to the top left BNC REF. VIDEO connector.

3. Slide the VIDEO termination switch to OFF.

4. Slide the REF VIDEO termination switch to ON, unless you're hooking something else up to reference video.

Editing

*Avid on a laptop:
Sony VAIO,
DSR-PD150 and
Xpress DV*

I got my first break in the business working on staff at Mel London's
production company. In between shooting, I was assigned to the editing
department, run by the legendary Irv Oshman. They had just purchased a
KEM, the flatbed film editing machine the size of a large dining room
table, with internal electro-mechanical timing belts, prisms and sprockets
that could only have been built by former cuckoo-clock manufacturers. Irv
was a brilliant editor, but loved his coffee. Unfortunately for me, he often
spilled much of the coffee into the KEM, and one of my added assignments
was an almost daily cleaning of its innards.

My other job was bin-diving. The film was organized into bins, which
looked like laundry-hampers with shower curtains. Instead of a curtain,
the film was hung up on sharp pins that protruded from the horizontal
cross-piece suspended above. On a large project, bins were organized by
subject, such as interiors, exteriors, interviews, explosions, or by scene.
The film was then assembled from the bins of selected takes into
sequences. These were then refined, cut, spliced, trimmed and re-
trimmed. Sometimes a trim would involve cutting out one frame of film.
This single, often crucial, frame would inevitably be needed several days
later, at which time it would also inevitably be learned that it had fallen
into the Stygian depths of one of the bins.

It is good for a cinematographer to know how to edit, because knowing
about transitions, divisions, scenes and continuity can only help improve

skills. Although a wag once said "anything cuts" (it might have been Orson Welles himself), certain shots definitely cut better than others. It is also good that the nice folks at Avid took the flatbed film editing analogy and developed the revolutionary nonlinear editing software most of us use today, forever offering a more comfortable alternative to bin diving.

Editing software comes in all sizes, flavors and prices. Many can be downloaded from the web as free demos. Some programs are software only—Avid Xpress DV and Final Cut Pro, MGI's Video-Wave and Ulead's VideoStudio; some come with an IEEE 1394 card, such as Pinnacle System's StudioDV or Digital Origin's IntroDV; and some come bundled with the computer you buy, like Apple iMacs and Sony VAIOs.

There are basically three flavors of interface—the way the software looks. Storyboard editing starts with a row of empty boxes. You drag each scene into a different box. You see the first frame of each take. It sort of looks like an arrangement of 3" x 5" still photos arranged in a row. You can change the order of events by swapping and sliding pictures around. Windows Movie Maker and Apple iMovie are storyboard based.

Timeline editing shows the various video and audio tracks as a graphic representation. Dragging each shot onto the timeline shows where it appears relative to other shots. Higher end programs switch quickly from timeline to storyboard views, and often combine a hybrid of both. Avid, Final Cut Pro, Media 100 and Cinestream are examples of this.

Text view shows statistics and descriptions of shots.

Let's start with the simplest way to chop up your footage, and work our way up. We'll begin with the free programs that come with Macs and Sony VAIOs.

Apple iMovie comes free with most Macs, iMacs, iBooks and Powerbooks. It and the advertising campaign that heralded its appearance were the "killer aps" that made DV what it is today. It's simple, and it works. I wouldn't cut a feature with iMovie—but it's good for assembling your sample reel, cutting a short subject or learning editing fundamentals. Suggestion: save your project, and then export it to a QuickTime file.

Not to be outdone, Microsoft hurriedly bundled Windows Movie Maker with Windows ME. It is easy to load DV footage, but useful only for the most rudimentary tasks like sending email movies. Footage is saved in the Windows Media Video Format, which is less than intuitive.

If you have a Sony VAIO computer, laptop or tower, it comes with DVgate Motion Capture, which is similar to its still capture cousin. (Don't bother with DVGate Assemble or Movie Shaker.) The DVCAM group advises against its use, because of a tendency for it to drop frames. If you have DVGate Still, exit the program before trying to capture motion video, and don't use it as a default extension in Adobe Premiere.

Exporting to Quicktime

Once you have exported your iMovie to QuickTime, you can change the file size if it's larger than you'd like. Although there are special programs like Media Cleaner 5, the QuickTime on your Mac or PC will do an adequate job of making files smaller. But first you need QuickTime Pro. It's a simple online upgrade if you have the free version of QuickTime. Go to *Edit, Preferences, Registration*, and click *Register Online.* The nice thing about QuickTime is that it works on both PC and Mac.

Open the QuickTime file (*file, open*). It will have a .moov or .mov extension.

Next, choose *file, export*. Click in the box next to *Export*: Select *Movie to QuickTime Movie.*

Click *options* (on the right side). Click *settings* under video. Choose *Sorenson Video* (because it's the best.) Pick *Medium Quality, 30 Frames per Second, Key Frame every 60 frames.* Use 320 x 240 for size. No filters.

Check your sound settings: *Qdesign Music 2, 44.100 kHz, Mono, 16 bit.*

Check *Prepare for Internet Streaming* and *Fast Start.* Then click *OK.* Give the file a name, and click *Save.* A 30 second piece of video, with audio, at 320 x 240, should compress to about 4 Megabytes—a decent size to send by email or post on the web.

Simple Boards and Software

What if your PC doesn't have an IEEE 1394 port? Well, you could buy a new Mac or Sony VAIO, since the Mac comes with FireWire and the VAIO comes with an i.LINK connection to the mother board. Or you can buy a IEEE 1394 PCI card, most of which come with some kind of editing software.

Try to get software with batch capture and logging—a process in which you mark the beginning and end of each shot you want downloaded into your computer and type a brief description of the shot. After you have finished logging, the computer automatically goes back and captures your selected takes.

Pinnacle Express DV, DV200

For around $79, you get FireWire/IEEE 1394 on your PC with Pinnacle Systems' Express DV (www.pinnaclesys.com). It not only enables you to capture and edit DV/DVCAM, burn the output to CD or DVD, but also lets you add FireWire hard drives and other peripherals. Pinnacle Studio DV adds a few more features.

Pinnacle Systems' DV200 is $329—which is cheaper than buying the Adobe Premiere 6 software that comes with it. DV200 has two external and one internal IEEE-1394 connectors. The card features DV CODEC technology from Sony. Runs on Windows 95, 98, Me, and 2000.

ADS PYRO

ADS (www.adstech.com) has a wide offering of PYRO PCI boards and PCMCIA cards. This has to be one of the cheapest ways to add 3 IEEE 1394 ports to the PCI slot of your PC. ADS Technologies PYRO BasicDV costs around $70, and includes Video Studio 4.01 and Photo Explorer for Windows. This is the card recommended by AVID for XpressDV. (www.adstech.com)

ADS has a $130 PCMCIA card for laptops, providing two FireWire ports.

IntroDV 2.0 and CineStream (previously EditDV)

As we write, Autodesk and Discreet have acquired Digital Origin's IntroDV, CineStream, and its predecessor EditDV. IntroDV is an inexpensive, PC-only introduction to DV, that usually comes bundled with an IEEE 1394 card. CineStream is for Mac or PC, and edits Windows Media, Real, MPEG-1, or QuickTime.

Serious Editing

A few years ago, serious editing meant a turnkey system of proprietary or highly modified hardware bundled with software. It usually involved buying the entire system from one place: computer, boards, software and tech support. The system could wind up costing more than a luxury car. Avid became the market leader in nonlinear editing, followed by Media 100, Softimage, Lightworks, FAST and others.

If you shoot or edit for a living, time wasted installing incompatible cards and resolving hardware conflicts can be more expensive than the extra cost of buying an all-in-one editing system. Anyone who has ever tried upgrading from Windows 95 to 98, or 98 to ME, knows the agony of hours spent on hold trying to reach intelligent signs of life at tech support. Although the simple boards and software described earlier will work, sooner or later you'll be lusting after something more serious, more powerful, faster and more professional.

For serious DVCAM/DV editing, it is now a close race between Avid's Xpress DV on the PC platform, and Apple Final Cut Pro on the Mac. Adobe Premiere is the third major contender, available on both platforms. I think it mostly comes down to the system and interface with which you're most familiar, and whether you want to use a Mac or Windows computer. They all handle NTSC or PAL.

There may be a new kid on the block. Sony's XPRI is currently targeted as an HD nonlinear editing system, but I wouldn't be too surprised if we see a DVCAM version soon, on VAIO laptops and towers. XPRI already comes in two configurations—Standard (SD) and High (HD) Definition. XPRI software runs under Windows 2000, on boards developed by Sony for HD throughput and processing. The editing interface is familiar, with source, record, timeline and bin windows. Stay tuned.

Serious Software

Avid Xpress DV, Apple Final Cut Pro and Adobe Premiere are all native DVCAM/DV nonlinear editing software packages that can be purchased alone, without hardware. They all cost less than the radio in the luxury car that originally set us back the same amount as an early Avid Media Composer. They all run on laptops or desktops, and handle NTSC or PAL projects. Having said all that, you still should consider who's going to be giving you technical support—because you will certainly want help when it's midnight, your palms are sweaty, the deadline is hours away, everything has locked up, and the client is wondering whether it's the end of his, or your, career.

Avid Xpress DV 2.0

Avid Xpress DV 2.0 brings Avid editing to laptops and desktops equipped with Windows 2000. The only additional piece of hardware required is an inexpensive ($80) IEEE 1394/Firewire/i.Link card. Avid has a list of "qualified" notebooks and desktops that have been tested. (www.avid.com)

As stand-alone software, Xpress DV has a list price of $1,699. Bundled with an IBM Intellistation or Dell tower, it can cost as little as $4,500. The compelling advantage of Xpress DV is that 90% of professional editing is done on Avids, and a low-cost compatible system can be very useful. It shares the familiar interface of other Avid products, and projects can be imported and exported between them.

New features in the latest version include dual monitor support (workstations only). There are 80 built-in effects, one-step export to Media Cleaner EZ and 16:9 widescreen support. Xpress DV has 4 video tracks (nestable for unlimited tracks), EDL support, Batch digitizing, IEEE 1394 and RS-422A deck control, and DVCAM camera compatibility with Sony. Audio editing handles 8 tracks with real-time mixing and real-time equalizing options.

The user interface is customizable, with a mappable keyboard and command palette, resizable source monitor, and configurable timeline toolbar. For output, there is a "Create DVD" command and Sonic AuthorScript for direct MPEG 1 & 2 output.

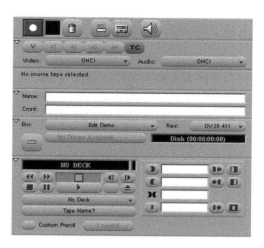

For another $1,300, you can add an additional software package called PowerPack, which includes Avid FilmScribe with Matchback, Script-Based Editing, Commotion, and Image Stabilize to correct shaky camera work.

Xpress DV has an extremely unique and helpful feature for DVCAM-to-film projects: Dupe-Detection in the Timeline. It alerts video-based editors to the unexpected and painful realization that any duplicate material in a film project will cost major dollars. This feature updates as the editor is working, flagging right in the timeline all duplicate material being used in the sequence; several colors also help flag various re-uses of frames or shots. The amount of duplicate handles can be set by user. Of course, Dupe-Detection works for video projects as well.

Another essential tool, that I think only exists on Xpress DV, is Keynumber display above Source/Record monitors. The film's edge-numbers can be displayed, which becomes important when cutting material shot on film, transferred to tape (video dailies).

Script-based editing allows direct editing from an imported script; takes can be grouped and looped for playback and evaluation, colors can be assigned to takes and takes can be "lined." This is not only for dramatic projects, but also used often on corporate, commercial and infomercial projects.

I would expect to see a Real Time rendering solution for Xpress DV by NAB 2002, along with uncompressed video options.

Apple Final Cut Pro 2.0

Final Cut Pro has quickly grown in popularity and usage, and with the latest upgrade, v2.0, Apple has addressed media-management issues and incorporated feedback from its loyal users. A "cutting-station mode" streamlines the User Interface for the bulk of editing features, and almost every setting in Final Cut Pro is customizable.

The User Interface is unique among nonlinear editing systems, and while it follows the source-record monitors workflow overall, many people feel it incorporates a lot of the key-framing options you would find in graphics programs. It uses keyframes directly in the clips being edited, both for audio and video manipulation. In Avid, you need to enter various modes (Effect Mode, Audio mode, etc to access keyframing.

Since Final Cut Pro uses Quicktime media, there's a good level of flexibility when importing and exporting material between programs.

The low cost of the program, combined with much faster laptops have helped Final Cut Pro become popular in projects ranging from television documenaries to Imax films. Final Cut Pro also incorporates software from FilmLogic, which allows frame-accurate cutlist creation, for film-originated projects.

3rd party hardware, including Matrox RT and ProMax, as well as software solutions, enable a large range of real-time effects; .

Apple Final Cut Pro runs on G4 Mac computers and Powerbook laptops. You can now use external FireWire drives, IDE or SCSI hard drives.

Features in Final Cut Pro include match frame editing, sequence trimming and batch recapture, scriptable effects, JKL navigation controls (K=stop, L=play forward, J=play backward), support for 16:9 picture aspect ratio, FilmLogic option for 24fps Cut, Pull and Optical Lists and other helpful editing tools. A feature enables clips to be automatically created whenever it detects a camera start or stop.

With Final Cut Pro, you can work with opacity control, motion blur and After Effects compatible plug-ins. Photoshop files can also be imported—maintaining their layers.

Final Cut Pro handles DV-based video as well as 2:1 compressed M-JPEG. Standard-definition (SD) and high-definition (HD) video can be edited with after-market boards, such as Pinnacle Cinéwave (similar to Pinnacle 3000 for PC), which use an external breakout box.

Uncompressed video, including HDTV support, can also be incorporated through hardware from Aurora systems (www.auroravideosys.com). They also provide a 24-fps editing solution for Final Cut Pro called IgniterFilm.

Most of these boards are tethered to a breakout box, which provides all the connectors and receptacles for the different video and audio I/O. The Pinnacle 3000 board for PCs (at right) looks the same as their Cinéwave board for Mac.

Adobe Premiere 6

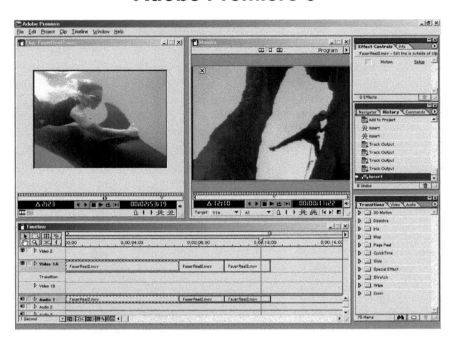

Adobe Premiere 6.0 is for Windows (98, ME) or Mac. In its earlier iterations, it was mostly used by web and CD authors, and was developed by some of the people who went on to work for Apple Final Cut Pro. The latest release, 6.0, addresses a criticism shared by many editors—that it had a corporate audio-visual "feel," as opposed to a filmmaker's tool.

It works pretty seamlessly with other Adobe programs like After Effects and Photoshop. You probably wouldn't want to cut a feature on it, but it will be fine for short subjects, commercials, music videos and web films. Premiere supports both IEEE 1394 and analog video. Its device drivers let you pick from a list of cameras and decks.

Most editing functions can be done directly in the timeline. Premiere 6.0 has a history palette like Photoshop's. Premiere 6.0 comes with Media Cleaner 5 EZ, to compress your project to QuickTime or Windows AVI.

Batch-capture operates similarly to Avid and Final Cut Pro. You mark in and out points on the DV tape. Then, a button in the Batch Capture window plays the tape back and imports the selected shots.

Premiere 6 saves window positions and sizes, like Photoshop and Illustrator. The history palette graphically displays recent actions so you can easily undo and redo them. Unlike Photoshop, however, Premiere 6 does not automate tasks.

Matchback

My good friend, editor and filmmaker Howard Phillips deserves single card credit for editing and proofreading this book, and contributed this page on Matchback.

With Matchback, a filmmaker may elect to have the footage tranferred to DVCAM to edit on FCP or Xpress DV. Both of these NLE (non linear editing) options offer tools to generate accurate negative cutlists from video-based editing projects.

Matchback can be briefly described as a method of matching back the durations an editor has created in his or her 30fps edit system to film's 24fps durations. It's sometimes described as converting a video EDL into a film cutlist, which is also true. Matchback programs are designed to incorporate film-based input, such as the OCN's (original camera negative's) keykode numbers and track them in 30fps-based editing systems like Xpress DV, Final Cut Pro and Premiere.

Avid has been doing this the longest, and their option is called FilmScribe. FilmScribe allows basically unlimited video tracks, and depending on the DVCAM project's budget, unlimited effects. FilmScrbe will generate all the types of lists required by negative cutters,as well as the Optical houses, where effects such as image-blow-ups, or motion effects and supers are created.

Apple works with FilmLogic, which uses a differrent method to arrive at converting a video EDL into a film cutlist; FilmLogic also can generate a range of different cutlists required for a film release.

There are other programs that allow you to edit your projects at 30fps (29.97) NTSC, or at 25fps if you're working in PAL, and then convert the timecode information into film-based footage & frames for negative cutters. Slingshot (from Trakker Technologies) is one such program, and can be used with Premiere, as well as Final Cut Pro and other NLE systems. Such programs also track use of duplicate material and describe optical-effects to be created.

Serious Boards

Matrox RTMac

Matrox RTMac is an add-on board for Mac G4 towers, developed through close cooperation between Matrox and Apple. It is optimized for Final Cut Pro, and adds analog composite and S-video (Y/C) input and output to Power Mac G4 computers, which already have Apple FireWire connections built in. With the RTMac's external breakout box, you can digitize source material from analog devices to use in your DV editing projects and record your finished projects to analog videotape for distribution. You also get full resolution viewing on a PAL or NTSC video monitor without connecting a DV device to your Power Mac G4. Dual-screen editing is an added benefit of Matrox RTMac. The RT Mac card lets you work with three layers of video and graphics in real time and create effects instantly—without rendering delays while working (effects still have to be rendered when outputting to tape). Rendering is the time spent while the computer processes complex video and audio effects, such as titles, dissolves, fades and so on. Street price is around $999.

Matrox RT2500

The RT2500 by Matrox is a comparable board for the PC, bundled with Adobe Premiere, Sonic DVDit! LE DVD and more. A breakout box provides IEEE 1394, composite and S-Video input and output. This system competes with Pinnacle's DV500 for realtime Windows DV and DVCAM editing, 4:3 and 16:9 native formats, DVD authoring and web streaming. Street price is around $999.

Pinnacle DV500 PLUS

$899 buys you a single PCI Card with IEEE 1394 and analog connectors for DV Editing With Real-time Effects, Titles and Filters. Real-time editing with connectors for both analog and digital (IEEE 1394) inputs and outputs. Input analog or digital video sources. Windows 2000/NT/Me/98SE/98. It includes Adobe Premiere 6.0, Minerva Impression for CD-R & DVD authoring, Pinnacle Systems' FreeFX and Hollywood FX Copper for 3D transitions and TitleDeko for titling. DV500 PLUS is a real-time editing package that takes full advantage of all Adobe Premiere 6.0 capabilities with professional quality features such as real-time multi-track audio mixer for volume adjustments, 16:9 widescreen effects, and image correction for color and brightness.

DV/DVCAM Compression

DV/DVCAM compression is 5:1. Compression is done by the hardware. It looks for adjacent pixels with the same colors that take up a lot of space, and assigns them mathematical values. Unlike software compression (QuickTime) and variable rate hardware compression (Avid AVR75— which was around 3:1), hardware compression of DV/DVCAM is fixed. This results in a better image. With variable compression, complex scenes sometimes have more grain or jagged "artifacts" than simple scenes. (A complex scene would be one with a lot of detail, like trees against a blue sky. A simple scene would be a close-up of a face.)

How Many Hard Drives Do I Need?

DV FireWire/IEEE 1394 requires 240 Megabytes of hard drive space per minute. Here's a brief chart to help calculate your storage requirements:

Running Time	Drive Space Needed
1 second	4 Mb
1 minute	240 Mb
10 minutes	2Gb
20 minutes	4 Gb
30 minutes	6 Gb
60 minutes	12 Gb
90 minutes (feature—final cut)	18 Gb
120 minutes (2 hours)	24 Gb
20 hours (feature—dailies)	240 Gb

Recent improvements make FireWire drives the easiest external add-on option. SCSI or IDE drives will also work, of course.

Uncompressed

For comparison, note that uncompressed QuickTime requires about 1.3 Gigabytes per minute and a throughput rate of 22-30 megs per second. Uncompressed Avid is about the same.

Where Does It All Go?

Your opus is complete. Where can it go? DV Tape, Analog Tape, Web, QuickTime, Windows Media, Real Player, CD, DVD, Film, Festivals and Theatrical Release.

The fastest way to release your DVCAM project is to eject it from the camera and hand it over to the police officer who is towering above you and inquiring why you are working without a permit on private property in full view of the "No Trespassing" signs.

The next higher level of distribution is copying it to another tape. Using a direct FireWire connection from one camcorder or deck to another, your tape can be "cloned" onto another tape. Analog audio and video outputs or S-Video connections let you copy your DVCAM to non-digital tapes, such as VHS, 3/4", Betacam SP and so on.

Farther up the evolutionary chain, nonlinear DV/DVCAM editing on a computer opens up vast possibilities and many choices of formats, compressions and destinations.

Apple's iDVD lets you "burn" your completed video to a standard DVD, which can be viewed by anyone with a standard DVD-equipped TV or computer. In the old days, up to the year 2000, it could take as long as 25 hours to record one hour of video to DVD. Apple's SuperDrive reduces that time to two hours. The iDVD software facilitates importing iMovie or any QuickTime file and making menus.

DVCAM to Film

Even though DVCAM distribution promises a surfeit of formats in numerous venues, the holy grail, the Everest, the promised land of DVCAM distribution is theatrical release on film.

And there's the paradox. The medium that vies with film for attention and economy still aspires to ultimate release on film.

The reasons, like almost everything else economic, are fear and greed. Greed, because most movie theatres and film festivals around the world use 35mm film projectors that have been paid for long ago.

Fear, because if they invest in a new digital computerized projection system today, they worry about its imminent obsolescence within eighteen months, replaced by something twice as good at half the price, as predicted by Moore's law.

Nevertheless, manufacturers are hard at work raising resolution and lowering prices on digital projection systems. But until a $100,000 digital projector becomes cheaper than the $3000 per print cost of a 90 minute feature on an already amortized projector in Poughkeepsie, you're probably going to have to "blow up" your DVCAM epic to 35mm film. Most theatres still project 35mm film. You don't shell out $10 for a ticket, along with concomitant popcorn and junk food, to watch DV in a theatre on a projection TV.

The machine looking like a freezer on wheels, pictured at right, is one of the devices that makes possible decent conversion of digital video to film.

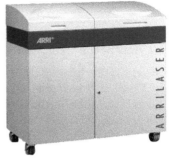

It works essentially like the laser printer attached to your computer. DVCAM data is "printed" frame by frame onto 35mm motion picture film, which becomes the new master.

It is safe to say that most of the material shot on DV and DVCAM will be viewed once, never be seen again, and soon relegated to the same dusty

ARRI Laser

drawer reserved for previous generations of home movie and video ephemera. There are the inevitable spools of 8mm film, and the projector whose burned-out bulbs aren't even available on eBay, and, of course, lots of Betamax tapes, because you were an early adopter of every superior technology, which did not guarantee its longevity or acceptance by everyone else.

Auteur Theory

I think anyone who ever picked up a movie or video camera has dreamed of becoming an auteur, darling of the film festivals, pursued by rival studios, loved by critics, adored by all.

Up to now, there have been a few surmountable impediments to such dreams, the most notable of which have been cost and crew.

Making movies is not cheap. Nor is it easy. François Truffaut once said that making a movie is like riding a stagecoach in the Wild West. You begin your journey with high expectations. Halfway through the journey, you just wish you had arrived at the destination. It's a complex process requiring a team of highly skilled people working together for long periods of time under difficult conditions. Truffaut also said, "if prisoners were forced to do what film crews willingly do, they'd rebel."

Enter the DVCAM

DVCAM is small, lightweight, fast and inexpensive. Almost anyone can use it—I regret to say, even without reading this book. The results may not look good, but there will most likely be an image. You will not wake up at three in the morning, in a cold sweat, wondering if you remembered to close the eyepiece during the remote-controlled stunt shot, or whether the entire scene has been irreparably fogged, because there are another six hours to go until dailies will be viewed at the lab. With DVCAM, what you see is what you get.

The other DVCAM aphorism is "you can pay now or you can pay later." Meaning, you can spend big bucks now and shoot your independent feature on 35mm, or you can spare every expense now, and shoot it on DVCAM. You, or the major studio that has just purchased worldwide distribution rights, can pay later to blow the DVCAM material up to 35mm.

And that is why there is so much excitement about this format. Most first film

ARRI Laser film gate

efforts are like first novels. They are put in square cans so they don't roll off the shelf where they remain in unappreciated obscurity.

But there is always the exception, and that is what we all dream of.

Low Budgets

How much does it cost to make a 90 minute, low budget feature? That's sort of like asking "how much does it cost to build a house?" For the purposes of comparison, let's say there are no above-the-line costs; director, producer, actors are all doing it as a labor of love. All production services have been donated, along with grip, electric and sound equipment. We'll only budget for actual shooting costs, and pretend it's a four-week shoot. A lot of numbers are rounded out and approximated for easy math. We're assuming a 10:1 shooting ratio, that you're buying real filmstock instead of recans, and you're making a workprint to view dailies (more expensive but highly recommended because it's the only way to see if that critical shot really was in focus).

Shoot on DVCAM

4 weeks	DVCAM camcorder rental	1000 - 1600 / week	$ 4,000 (you could almost buy the camera for this price)
15 hours (900 mins)	DVCAM tape	$ 35 / hour (about .60 / min)	$ 525
			total $ 4,525

Shoot on 35mm Film

4 weeks	35mm camera rental	4,000 / week	$ 16,000 (another $ 60,000 might buy you an old ARRI 35BL3 system
15 hours (900 mins)	35mm film, processing, work-print	$100 / minute (90 x 1000' rolls)	$ 90,000
			total $ 106,000

Shoot on 16mm Film

4 weeks	16 mm camera rental	3,000 / week	$ 12,000 (another $ 8,000 might buy you an old ARRI 16SR system)
15 hours (900 mins)	16mm film, processing, work-print	$35 / minute (90 x 400' rolls)	$ 31,500
			total $ 43,500

Peddling the Project

So far, shooting on DVCAM has saved you $101,475 compared to 35mm, and $38,975 compared to 16mm.

Next, you need to find a distributor—a search conducted by word of mouth and by sending video dubs of the project to various companies. You enter some of the festivals that accept video. But, you soon discover how difficult it is to find a buyer of your video. You decide to plunge forward, spend the big bucks, and enter some of the major festivals.

For that, you now begin the process of DVCAM to 35mm film. Here are some ballpark figures—they are constantly changing, and often negotiable.

DVCAM to 35mm Film Costs

Method	Cost	Total for 90 minutes
Laser Film Printer	$550-750 / minute (3000-4000 / minute on spots and shorts)	$ 50,000
Electron Beam Recorder	$ 395 - 900 / minute	$ 36,000
Swiss Effects		$ 33,000
Kinescope	$ 230 / minute	$ 20,700

DVCAM to 16mm Film

Method	Cost	Total for 90 minutes
Kinescope	$ 75 / min	$ 6,750

Since we're trying to spare every expense, as my producer friend Mel London used to say, transferring from DVCAM to 16mm using a Kinescope is the cheapest. For around $75 per minute, you get a color negative and timed composite release print along with sound.

16mm to 35mm Blowup

9,000 feet (90 minutes)	$ 5 / foot	$ 45,000 - 50,000

If you subsequently find that a festival will only accept 35mm prints, you're back in major spending mode. Blowups from 16mm to 35mm average around $5 per foot, based on the final 35mm footage (90 minutes at 90 feet/minute=8100 feet). That will total around $50,000 for a 90 minute show, once you add extra cost of leader and a few other things, including interpositive, interneg and composite check print with sound.

DVCAM to Film Transfers

Laser Film Recorder (Printer)

The big names in laser "printing" systems are ARRI, Eastman Kodak (Cineon Lightning), Digital Cinema Systems (Lux) and Pthalo Systems (Verité). These are commonly used in big budget, effects-heavy major motion pictures. The original 35mm negative is often scanned into a "sister" companion laser scanner at high resolution. The digital

ARRI Laser

image is then manipulated, composited, matted or keyed, and the final product goes back to film via the laser film printer, at a rate of about three to six seconds per frame. Light from the laser exposes a fine-grain internegative (5244) film, whose ASA is around 1. The native rate is 4K resolution, with a 2K option. The laser does not use lenses, and works somewhat like your home computer laser printer.

CRT Film Printer

Slower and sometimes cheaper than laser printers, Cathode Ray Tube (CRT) devices use a film camera to shoot three consecutive exposures on each frame (through red, green and blue filters) of a high resolution monochromatic monitor. They are made by Management Graphics (Solitaire) and Celco. It takes about five to forty seconds per frame at 2 or 4K resolution.

Swiss Effects

Swiss Effects is a company in Zurich that has devised a proprietary CRT technology. It is a popular spot to convert features shot on DVCAM into film. Its appeal is a combination of speed and personal attention. Standard definition DVCAM is "up-rezzed" (increased resolution) to 2K on the fly, and recorded at rates of 5 seconds per frame. Native 2K images, either from HD or 35mm film, is recorded at .7 to 2 seconds per frame. They can use different camera negative films, such as 5245, instead of traditional print and intermediate stocks. Each frame is exposed three times, but at a much faster rate than other CRTs. So, while other machines are still chugging along at three to six seconds per frame and the deadline is looming for your film festival premiere, Swiss Effects is akin to FedEx—absolutely, positively getting it there on time.

Electron Beam Recorder

Electron Beam Recorders (EBRs) use a method similar to the way electron beams scan the phosphors on the back of a TV screen. EBRs use electron beams to expose black and white film. Three passes are made: red, green and blue, something like the old Technicolor 3 strip process. The three strips are printed in three passes back to color film through color filters. Most EBRs are 16mm, except Sony's, and require a blowup to 35mm. Most agree that this technology will be obsolete soon.

Kinescope

Kinescopes are as old as live television, when there were video cameras, but video tape had not yet been invented. Many of the early shows were recorded directly onto film with a kinescope, which was basically a black and white NTSC video monitor photographed by a motion picture camera. Ironically, most of these kinescoped shows have survived better than the early video tapes, which suffered from demagnetization or dropouts.

I suppose if you were really desperate and broke, you could improvise your own kinescope by having your cousin the film student borrow a camera and shoot your own screen. It would look horrendous, but it would certainly be cheap.

2K - 4K Resolution

When you discuss laser film printers and scanners, talk inevitably revolves around 2K or 4K scans. They refer to digital resolution of 2000 or 4000 pixels per horizontal line, and the difference is a matter of time and money. It costs more to work at 4K because it takes the machine longer to do the work.

The image in video is made up of pixels; film consists of light-sensitive, microscopic (.003 to .0003mm) grains of silver halide crystals, arranged in layers that take on colors when processed.

The more pixels there are, the greater the detail. That's why a Megapixel digital still camera looks better than one shooting at 640 x 480.

The finer the grain of motion picture film, the sharper and more detailed it looks. That's why Kodak EXR-50D 5245, a 50 ASA film stock, looks sharper and richer than Kodak Vision 800T 5289, an 800 ASA stock, and Kodak internegative 5244, with an ASA of about 1, is even sharper.

A frame of NTSC video consists of approximately 307,200 pixels, and a PAL frame has about 368,640 pixels.

The image on a frame of film is made by lots of little grains, not pixels. But, if we were to make a mathematical or analytical conversion, each frame of film would be 5000 x 3760 (18,800,000) pixels.

If we scanned a frame of film at 5000 x 3846 resolution, we would need 58Megabytes of storage space for that one frame (5,000 x 3,846 x 3 colors). That's 1.4 Gigabytes per second, which, at the moment is not easily manageable. So the image is scanned and printed at lower resolutions, usually 2K.

There has been much debate about the maximum resolution that can be seen by the human eye. Inevitably, the figure 2500 pixels is tossed about. Problem is, it depends where you're sitting in the movie theatre. The industry standard is to watch from a distance that is 1 1/2 screen widths away from the screen. (If the screen is 60 feet wide, you sit 90 feet away.) Not fair! How far away were you during the time warp sequence in *2001: A Space Odyssey*? I'll bet you were in the front row, like me.

Keeping DVCAM to Film in Mind

What does all this mean?

It means plan ahead. If you are going to shoot an independent low-budget feature on DVCAM, prepare for all contingencies in advance.

1. Shoot tests. Do a test of the DVCAM-to-film system you'll be using.

3. Get prices in advance.

4. Know the aspect ratio of your release print (1.33:1, 1.66:1, 1.78:1, 1.85:1) and frame accordingly while shooting. You can cut a piece of gray neutral density gel to serve as a frame line in your viewfinder.

5. On the Sony DSR-500WS, shoot in 16:9. On the other models, I suggest the 4:3 aspect ratio with an anamorphic adapter.

6. Do not use the digital zoom.

7. Optical image stabilizing (SteadyShot) is OK, and highly recommended.

8. Beware of strobing. If you pan too quickly in film, objects can look jittery. A rule of thumb, often broken, is to pan no faster than the time it takes for an object at one side of the frame to get to the other side. Whip pans are fine. They're supposed to be blurred.

9. Turn manual shutter to 1/60th second.

10. Use a separate tape recorder for audio, preferably DAT, as audio backup. Get as good a feed as possible to the camcorder. The DAT will be available for looping and special audio work. Use clapsticks at the beginning of each take, if possible. The editor will sing your praises daily.

11. The envelope please.

"Look"

The great debate between film and video always ends up in a discussion of contrast and what constitutes the special "look" of motion picture film compared with the special "look" of DVCAM. These questions constantly pop up on Internet discussion forums, including the one at www.cinematographer.com.

A number of companies offer effects and electronic plug-ins to try to make video look more like film. The analogy, I'm afraid, is somewhat similar to making a watercolor look like an oil painting. We are working with two different formats, with different brushes and palettes. I don't think that the "look" of motion picture film is determined by the fact that it is running at 24 frames per second. Run the same film at 30 fps, and it still looks like film. Furthermore, the argument that the unique "look" of film is created by the inherent grain pattern is refuted by watching an IMAX film. You can't see the grain in the 70mm print.

So what is the "look" of film and what is the "look" of DVCAM? It's a complex combination of exposure, latitude, color, contrast, texture, detail and all kinds of other measurable and sometimes intangible or subliminal factors. Film currently has a wider range of exposure latitude than DVCAM. You can see details in the dark shadows. You can simultaneously see details in the highlights. Imagine you're filming a dark room with a window, and trees outside. Film would allow you to see the cat on the rug, and the bird in the tree outside the sunlit window. In DVCAM, we may not have as much range of exposure latitude, but there's other magic going on. If we forego the highlights, DVCAM may see into low-light areas in ways that film cannot. The tree outside the window may be overexposed. But we'll see detail in the cat's fur even when it's hiding under the sofa.

Using Sony's DSR-PD150, I noticed it handled a contrast range far beyond what we expected from its specs. The DSR-500WS and the other high-end DVCAM camcorders have additional digital signal processing systems, like DynaLatitude, that adjust the camera's management of highlight areas in the scene. Their high sensitivity and low noise provides clean detail and low noise in darkly shadowed areas. They can, with appropriate adjustment, do a credible job with the overexposed areas at the same time, in the same shot. In the way that an advanced telecine can change the characteristic curve of your exposed negative, electronic circuits in current camcorders have changed my preconceived notions about previous generations of video and contrast.

What does this mean for the cinematographer lighting a scene for DVCAM? While acknowledging the pitfalls of over-simplification, it suggests shifting exposure more to the highlights—stopping down more than one would for film. We might use more ND gel on windows, or art-direct the scene so overexposed highlights are less prominent. We should be aware that kickers or backlights that look radiant on film might look better when scrimmed down a little for DVCAM. As always, nothing replaces thorough testing, following through to final release. We want to be sure the lighting that looks wonderful on the monitor during the shoot will be equally stunning when transferred by laser, for example, to film and projected on the largest movie screen. We find, as we become more familiar with the digital adjustments provided in the higher-end DVCAM camcorders, that we can create our own interesting compromises in handling dark, shadowed areas along with overexposed areas in the same shot.

Depth of Field

One of the main things to consider when using DVCAM for theatrical release on film is depth of field. One of the immutable laws of optics is that the smaller the image area, the greater the depth of field. Depth of field is a measurement of how much of the scene is in focus.

Let's say you're filming a mouse sitting in the middle of a staircase, and let's assume the mouse will hold still for the entire duration of your experiment. Maybe it's a stuffed mouse. You are using a 100m lens at T2.8. You are shooting with a 35mm motion picture camera. You focus on the mouse. The stair steps immediately above and below the mouse will appear sharp.

To get more stair steps in focus, you can change a number of variables. Stop the lens down to T11. The more you close down the iris, the more depth of field. Or you can zoom wider. The wider the lens, the more depth of field. Another way to get more depth of field is to use a 16mm camera, or a DVCAM or DV camcorder. The smaller the image area, the greater the depth of field, and the more everything will appear to be in focus.

"What's wrong with that?" you ask. Nothing. But that's one of the main differences in look between film and video, and no amount of post effects that seek a "look" of film can change depth of field.

One of the distinctive qualities of 35mm motion picture photography is its usually shallow depth of field. In essence, the camera selectively focuses on an area, putting emphasis on it. Backgrounds tend to become "soft." 16mm film has more depth of field, and 8mm even more.

There is an exception: *Citizen Kane*. Everything is in focus. Gregg Toland, the Director of Photography, used lenses closed down almost to pinholes and so much light that reporters joked that exposure could have been measured with a thermometer instead of a lightmeter.

Why DVCAM usually looks better than DV

Most consumer DV camcorders use 1/4" chips, as does the DSR-PD100A. Sony's DSR-PD150 and DSR-250 camcorders use 1/3" CCD chips, which are larger. The DSR-300A uses 1/2" CCD chips, which are the same size as a 16mm film frame. So material shot with the DSR-300A will have about the same depth of field as a 16mm film camera. The DSR-500WS uses 2/3" chips, which are slightly larger than a Super16 frame, and are the same size as high-end HD camcorders. As we mentioned before, the larger the chip, the less depth of field, the more selective focus will be.

It's no wonder that, when given the choice of DVCAM cameras, John Bailey, ASC shot *The Anniversary Party* with a DSR-500WS.

John Bailey, ASC on *Anniversary Party*

John Bailey, ASC, is a brilliant Director of Photography, whose impressive list of credits includes *Ordinary People*, *The Big Chill*, *Silverado* and *The Out-of-Towners*. His *Anniversary Party* is considered by many to be the gold standard by which other DVCAM features are currently measured. I spoke with him recently.

Q: Why DVCAM instead of film?

Bailey: It was a joint decision. The directors, Jennifer Jason Leigh and Alan Cumming, wanted to portray an upscale lifestyle, highly stylized, somewhat slick. Jennifer had done a Dogma film, *The King is Alive*, and liked the spontaneity. We then watched Bertolucci's *The Conformist*, as an example of a stylized, upscale film style.

Q: Why did it look so good?

Bailey: at every stage of the finishing, both the video and film, from online video mastering and film rendering, to film answer printing we had daily close contact with the facilities, Laser-Pacific, EFilm and Deluxe Labs. All were within a mile of each other and so the lines of communication were excellent.

Q: What camera did you use?

Bailey: The Sony DSR-500WS. I rated it at 250 or 320 ASA. I used my lightmeter, and filled by eye. Everything on the camera was on the manual settings. We adjusted the gain to -3 dB for richer blacks—like overexposing a negative. The hardest thing was taking light away, like a negative fill, because the camera is so sensitive in shadow areas. I had to reach for contrast.

Q: How did you achieve the look?

Bailey: While it doesn't have the resolution of Super16, I would say it was better than I'd ever hoped for. We did it by following through carefully all the way. Despite the limited exposure latitude compared with film. We were careful to set white balance all the time. This was not just "capturing," this was attention to consistent quality. It was shot in 19 days.

Q: Tell us about post.

Bailey: In finishing, we didn't use the DVCAM master. That was never touched. We used a clone assembled by the edit list. The clone was color-corrected on a 2K DaVinci and output to D-1, which EFilm then used to make the 35mm 5244 color internegative on their ARRI Laser Recorder. We spent a lot of time making field enhancements, softening certain pixels, and correcting the image of artifacts. My advice is, wherever you finish a DVCAM project, do it close by. Logistics are important. It takes time, and you want to be there.

Q: What about crew?

Bailey: We had a video engineer, with a wave form monitor and we used 3 reference monitors. A camera assistant for focus and so on.

Q: Is DVCAM a good tool for film schools?

Bailey: Yes, it's wonderful to use as a tool. But it's important to remember it's a tool in the service of an art form. Students should study paintings, and stay aware of art history. Anybody can turn on a camera and get an image. I'm tired of the word "capture"—it reminds me of catching butterflies or wild animals. But it demeans the notion of cinematography. We have to stay at the intersection of film and art. We have to pay attention to detail. There's nothing like being in a screening room, and the lights go down, and you see your work up there for the first time.

Theory

Origin of the Species

Digital Video includes DVCAM as well as DV, 24P, Digital Betacam, HD, Digital8, Digital S, DVCPRO, DVCPRO50 and DVCPRO100. DV is sometimes called DVC (Digital Video Cassette), and you'll still see some tapes labeled "DVC" on the package. The common thread among all these formats is that the video signal is stored in binary code: ones and zeroes. Analog video stores the information as waves that change in frequency and amplitude (think of an oscilloscope or waves in the ocean).

DV began as a 1/4" digital video format, originally designed for the consumer market, to replace Hi8. Like many previous tape formats, the consumer version caught the eye of professionals, and Sony adapted it for professional use by increasing track pitch and tape speed, and adding other refinements. DVCAM was Sony's faster, professional version of consumer DV.

Panasonic introduced its professional iteration of DV in 1995, and called it DVCPRO. Sony introduced DVCAM in 1996. It was almost reminiscent of the VHS-Beta style format wars. DVCAM shares the same size cassettes as DV. DVCPRO uses different cassettes: Medium and Large, no Mini.

The two formats basically use similar video and audio encoding schemes as the consumer DV format, but have different cassette sizes, along with slight differences in speed and track pitch. You can't always play one cassette in the other deck, although some decks have dual capability. DVCAM uses Advanced Metal Evaporated tape. DVCPRO uses Metal Particle tape.

Comparisons: DV, DVCAM, DVCPRO

The track width of DV is slightly smaller (10 microns) than DVCAM (15 microns) and DVCPRO (18 microns).

DV runs at a slightly slower speed (1/3 slower) than DVCAM, which runs slightly slower than DVCPRO.

DV runs at 18.81 mm per second (¾ inches per second in Standard (SP) mode, and 12.56 mm/s (½ ips) in Long Play (LP) mode.

DVCAM runs at 28 mm/sec, and DVCPRO at 33.82 mm/sec.

A "Standard" DVCAM cassette is the same size as a "Large" DVCPRO cassette. Standard and Large often become confused in catalogs.

I think the main ingredient for the success of DVCAM is the digital part of its name, and its seamless import and export to computers. The picture quality is better than Hi8 and just as good, if not better, than Betacam SP. Unlike analog formats, the image will not degrade as copies are made. It is much less prone to dropout, which plagued Hi8.

The tape is 1/4" (6.35 mm) wide, but usually called 6mm. I suppose that is to avoid confusion with 1/4" audio tape.

DVCPRO

Panasonic's DVCPRO (sometimes called D-7) uses metal-particle tape instead of metal evaporated tape. The track pitch is increased to 18 microns. Unlike DVCAM, the audio cue track and timecode control track of DVCPRO are recorded on two extra linear tracks.

The tape is transported at 34 mm/sec (DV is 17mm per second, DVCAM is 28 mm/sec.) Most DVCPRO VTRs, however, can play back DV, DVCAM, and DVCPRO tapes. An adapter is required for the Mini cassette.

Digital 8

Digital 8 was introduced by Sony in 1999. It has the same specifications as DV, but records onto the familiar Video8 - Hi8 cassette. The picture should look the same. The only drawback is that timecode cannot be sent over the i.LINK / IEEE 1394 cable. That becomes a serious drawback only if you plan to edit the tapes, and need to return to the original tape for frame-accurate re-editing.

The main reason to buy a Digital 8 camera is compatibility with all your old Video8 tapes. Digital 8 camcorders will play back the older format tapes. This involves multi-speed design, since Digital8 runs twice as fast as Hi8. Digital 8 camcorders are cheaper, but they're also bigger and bulkier. A 120 minute cassette will record 60 minutes in Digital8.

Digital S

Digital-S (called D-9) is JVC's format that delivers 50 Mbps of video data compressed at 3.3:1, with 4:2:2 sampling. This is similar to Digital Betacam, and some decks can play back your old S-VHS tapes. Remember, S-VHS and Betacam are both ½" formats

DVCPRO50

DVCPRO50 from Panasonic uses regular DVCPRO tape, but moves it faster to achieve a Mbps data rate. Compression is 3.3:1.

How DVCAM Camcorders Work

Through the Lens

In a DVCAM camcorder, light passes through the lens and hits tiny silicon particles on a computer chip, called a CCD for charged coupled device. This image sensor converts the light into an analog electrical signal that is sent to associated circuits, where it is converted to digital and compressed to make it smaller and more manageable.

Three Chip Cameras (3 CCDs)

With a few exceptions, most consumer DV camcorders use one CCD to gather picture information.

DVCAM camcorders use 3 chips. Each CCD handles one of the three primary colors: Red, Green and Blue. The light passing through the lens is separated into red, green and blue by a beam-splitting prism, and then each color is sent to its own CCD. This process provides better picture detail, more accurate color reproduction, a wider dynamic range and virtually no color noise.

This will change in time. As chips get better, achieving higher resolution and fidelity of color, there will no longer be a need to divide the work up among three separate chips. Shorter flange to chip distances can be used, and the millions of excellent still and motion picture lenses can be used.

Luminance and Chrominance

Black and white would consist of one channel: luminance, which means brightness. Absence of luminance (brightness), is black. Maximum brightness would be white. All the steps in between are the shades of gray. Chrominance is color.

Components

DVCAM is usually color. And it's component.

Component video breaks the video signal down into three separate "tracks," or "channels" of information. To save space on the video tape, the engineers took a shortcut. A video signal really should have at least five tracks: red, blue, green, brightness and contrast. But, by combining some of the information, they eliminated two of the five "tracks." The result is the Y, R-Y, B-Y scheme.

The three "tracks" of video information are:

1. Y (luminance, or brightness)
2. R-Y (Red color, or chrominance, minus the luminance signal)
3. B-Y (Blue color, or chrominance, minus the luminance signal).

The Red and Blue channels also carry some green color information. The Y signal is the largest of the three "tracks." In addition to brightness, it carries information about contrast, resolution and sharpness.

Composite Video

By the way, composite video is what you're probably watching on your TV set at home, along with VHS, Video 8, Hi8, 3/4" U-matic and 1". The signal is analog. All the picture information of color, brightness and contrast is lumped together, composited, on one "track" on the video tape.

DVCAM Components and Conversion

So the signal is divided into three components: Y, Y-R and Y-B. The next thing that happens inside your DVCAM camcorder is the analog to digital conversion, which is a three-part process consisting of sampling, quantization and digitizing.

Sampling

Sampling means how many times a second the signal is divided into millions of sections. The black and white component is sampled 13.5 million times a second (13.5 MHz). That means it is divided into 13.5 million sections. Sampling is a measurement of the speed at which the three components are checked for information. It's measured in

Megahertz, and the bigger the number, the faster the information is gathered. This measurement of speed is similar to the way your 100MHz computer pokes along much more slowly than your brand new 966 MHz Pentium or 733 MHz G4.

The big difference is that, in video, all the information has to come out 30 times a second, or 25 in PAL. So, if there's a bottleneck in the sampling, you don't get a picture. Your TV can't wait, fingers drumming, while the information is slowly being processed.

The Y component (luminance) of the DVCAM signal is sampled at 13.5 MHz, which means that the black and white (along with brightness and resolution) video signal is checked 13.5 million times a second. Each of the two color components (R-Y, B-Y) is sampled 3.375 million times a second (3.375 Mhz).

When you see the number 4:1:1, it is referring to the ratio of the luminance to the chrominance sampling (13.5 divided by 3.375 is 4).

Why so fast? Since there's more information in the Y component (luminance) than the other two—not only black and white but also shades of gray, level of picture detail, brightness and contrast—it has to be checked more often. Remember, all the information has to be read and translated into a digital stream.

4:2:2, 4:1:1, 4:2:0

D-1 and Digital Betacam encode the video signal at a ratio of 4:2:2. DVCAM encodes the signal at a ratio of 4:1:1 (4:2:0 in PAL).

These numbers are the ratios of the way the video signal is broken down into the three separate "tracks" of information.

When we say Digital Betacam is 4:2:2, and DVCAM is 4:1:1, we are comparing the different ratios of brightness to color information. The numbers don't actually refer to any real, absolute values. They are ratios. The numbers 4:1:1 could just as well be 8:2:2 or 16:4:4 or 1:¼:¼.

In 4:2:2, the first number, "4", refers to the 13.5 MHz luminance (brightness and green) sampling rate in the video signal. D-1, Digital Betacam, Betacam SX, Digital-S, DV, DVCAM and DVCPRO all sample at 13.5 MHz.

The second and third numbers in "4:2:2" or "4:1:1" are the ratios of the other two "tracks" of color information compared with the luminance "track."

So, 4:2:2 (D-1, Digital Betacam, Betacam SX, Digital-S, and DVCPRO50) means that the two "tracks" of color information are sampled at half the rate of the luminance, which would be 6.75 MHz.

4:1:1 (NTSC DV, DVCAM, DVCPRO) means that the color information is sampled at ¼ the rate of the luminance signal, or 3.375 MHz.

What this really means is that Digital Betacam and the 4:2:2 formats let us have 360 colors per horizontal scan line of video. DVCAM and the 4:1:1 formats let us have 180 colors per scan line. What, only 180 colors? But my computer displays millions of them.

Lest we become seriously panicked by this paucity of colors, remember that BetaSP, that venerable standard of the last twenty years, only has a color sampling rate of 1.5MHz. Although it's not digital, and the comparison is not totally accurate, Betacam SP would translate to a ratio of approximately 4:½:½.

No one ever said NTSC and PAL were great display formats. Each scan line is made up of 720 pixels (dots of color) going across the screen. And, as we've pointed out, although NTSC is supposed to scan 525 of these horizontal lines up and down, by the time it gets onto your TV set, it's far fewer. Figure on 480 pixels (dots of color) going up and down. That is certainly worse than your computer monitor.

Quantizing

Sampling tells us how often the three channels are being checked, but we also need to know about their quantities. Quantizing is the process of deciding how many colors and how much brightness we're going to see. You can adjust your computer to display 256 colors, thousands of colors, or millions of colors. Try it. Setting 256 colors will let the computer run faster. Millions of colors slows things down. The same holds true of our video signal. If we quantize too many colors, things will bog down, and our picture will be a blob.

The Y component is quantized as 256 shades of gray, ranging from pure white to deep black. The other two components, R-Y and B-Y, are quantized as 256 colors each. This is also called 8 bit depth. But, as we just read earlier in the discussion of 4:1:1, we're really only getting 180 colors, not 256.

Digitizing

Next, all this information has to be converted to binary file format, since DVCAM is, after all, digital. Every pixel will be represented by binary numbers, defining placement, color, brightness, and picture detail.

Compression

The technology that really makes digital video possible is the process of compression, in which the actual file size of each frame is made smaller by using mathematical formulas to describe areas of similar color or brightness. Let's say our picture has a big blue sky in it. Rather than define each pixel with the same numbers, compression schemes tell the file to repeat the same shade of blue, for example, for the next 20 horizontal pixels.

DVCAM images are compressed at a rate of 5:1. Here we go again with more ratios. DVCAM information travels back and forth from the camera to your computer or monitor at a constant digital "stream" of 35 Mbps (millions of bits per second), which is the same as 3.5 MB/ sec (Megabytes or Millions of bytes per second).

Think of your modem. A standard modem has a "bandwidth" of 56 Kbps, which lets information travel along at 56,000 bits per second, and a paltry 5,600 bytes per second (divide by 10). By comparison, the hard drive in your computer probably has a transfer rate of 5 Megabytes per second.

So, the signal is compressed to 1/5 of its original data size. Without compression, the camcorder and computer would have to stream data five times larger, at rates of 350 Mbps or 35 Megabytes per second. That's too fast even for most hard drives, whose average transfer rates are 8 Megabytes per second. Not to mention the size of video cassette we'd have to use.

Unlike JPEG, MPEG and other video compression schemes (called codecs) used on computers, the compression here is done by the hardware, so it's fast and consistent, not variable. NTSC DVCAM only has color in every other pixel. PAL DVCAM has color in every other line. That's how so much space is saved in DVCAM.

By the way, JVC's Digital-S (D-9) and Panasonic's DVCPRO50 is compressed 3.3:1, with a data rate of 50 Mbps (5 MB/sec). Sony's Digital Betacam is compressed 2:1.

Heads and Tape

Like most video systems, DVCAM tape is pulled along a rotating drum to which are attached two tiny electro-magnetic heads for recording and playing back video and audio. The heads are made of small coils of wire that magnetize the DVCAM tape when an electrical pulse is applied. Since it's digital, the pulse is either on or off. A zero is represented by absence of magnetizing. A one is represented by a magnetized portion of tape.

The drum, which is about an inch in diameter, rotates 150 times per second, 9,000 rpm. The drum is angled so that the heads travel in a diagonal direction along the width of the tape, laying down information in bands—called tracks—from top to bottom. This is called helical scanning.

Each time the head comes in contact with the tape, it records a "track." There are 10 tracks per frame of NTSC DVCAM (12 tracks in PAL). Each track contains picture information for approximately 48 video scan lines. Extra tracks are used for timecode and audio.

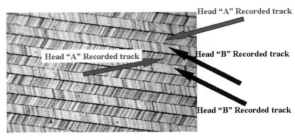

This is true micro-miniaturization. Each track on DVCAM tape is 15 microns wide (10 millionths of a meter). A human hair is 60 microns thick.

In the picture above, taken by Sony, we are looking at the actual bits of magnetized tape. A recording is made on the tape. A length of recorded tape is extracted and removed from the cassette. The length of recorded tape is attached to a jig and dipped in a series of magnetic solutions. Suspended magnetic material in the solution clings to the magnetized areas on the tape. This is the same principle used in school science class where iron filings show the magnetic field of a magnet. The developed recording is placed under a microscope and the actual recorded tracks are visible.

Azimuth recording is used to prevent cross talk. Each head records at opposite angles. That is why we see the tracks at different angles.

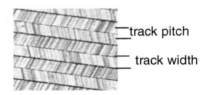

track pitch

track width

Each track contains Sub Code information, Video information, Audio and ITI (Insert and Track information). For NTSC, 10 tracks equals one frame. For PAL, 12 tracks equal one frame.

As stated at the beginning of the book, when DVCAM first arrived, most of us skeptics doubted that DVCAM tape was really better than DV tape. But as the wise man said, "you pay for what you get."

It turns out that DVCAM tape is indeed more durable, and can be archived for more than 30 years (ideally at 54-59°F, 27-32% humidity).

Durability
Variation of friction coefficient of DVCAM and DV tape

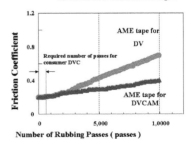

DVCAM tape is manufactured to higher tolerances for professional use. It has about 50% fewer dropouts than DV tape.

DVCAM tape has better physical stability—more resistance to stretching and shrinkage. Tape width is more uniform because slitting is done on more accurate machines.

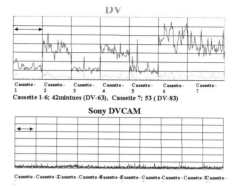

Audio

DVCAM uses digital audio, recorded onto the DVCAM tape as a digital signal, similar to a CD or DAT.

Sampling

As with the video signal, audio is sampled and quantized. The camcorder usually offers you a menu of sampling rates, typically 48 KHz, 44.1 KHz or 32 KHz. Sound is sampled at a much slower rate than video because there isn't as much information to gather. A 48 KHz sampling rate means the sound is checked 48,000 times a second. By the way, DAT (Digital Audio Tape) uses 48 KHz sampling and CDs use 44.1 KHZ sampling. The audio in the DVCAM format is not compressed.

Quantization

When setting up audio on your camcorder, you are sometimes offered the choice of 16 bit or 12 bit audio. This is the quantization, or quantity of choices being made while sampling.

Higher sampling and quantization rates will yield better sound. 48 KHz with 16 bit sound is the best. However, remember that 16 bit audio gives you two tracks of sound, while 12 bit audio lets you record 4 tracks. This should rarely be a problem until you start recording your son's string quartet, and want to isolate each instrument with a separate microphone.

16 bit

16 bit is 2 to the 16th power, which means there are 65,536 choices of tonal variation.

12 bit

12 bit is 2 to the 12th, which is 4,096. 12 bit audio is usually sampled at 32 KHz.

Comparing DVCAM with Digital Betacam

DVCAM camcorders work pretty much the same way as high-end digital camcorders like Digital Betacam. Both are component formats, which means the picture information is recorded onto tape as three separate "tracks." The three tracks separate out the three primary colors, along with brightness and contrast. The components are: brightness (luminance, Y), Red-Y (chrominance, R-Y) and Blue-Y (chrominance, B-Y).

By the way, S-Video is also a component format, but with only two "tracks" or channels of picture information. And composite video lumps everything together.

DVCAM has a sample rate of 13.5 MHz, which is the same as Digital Betacam.

However, Digital Betacam uses 4:2:2 encoding compared with DVCAM's 4:1:1 encoding.

Digital Betacam, therefore, will have truer color (chrominance), and a better signal-to-noise ratio (less grain or noise) because of its 10-bit encoding (1,024 colors) versus DVCAM's 8-bit (256 colors).

Digital Betacam compresses the signal 2:1, while DVCAM compresses it 5:1.

Comparing DVCAM with Betacam SP

Now, let's compare DVCAM with Betacam SP, which has been a broadcast, industrial and documentary standard for nearly twenty years. I think DVCAM is as good as, if not better than, analog Betacam SP.

DVCAM's video signal-to-noise ratio is 54 dB. Betacam SP is 51 dB.

DVCAM's luminance bandwidth is 5.75 MHz. Betacam SP is 4.1 MHz.

Recently, the good lenses of Betacam SP and Digital Betacam camcorders have become available on higher-end professional DVCAM cameras. And better glass is being used on the consumer models.

Image Stabilization

When you have a tiny camera, of no apparent weight, appended to your hand with a thin leather strap, every move you make and every breath you take will show up on screen in headache-inducing magnification.

The remedy for home-video induced nausea is image stabilization. There are two kinds: optical and digital. The idea is to shift the image in the opposite direction of the camera's movement. Suppose you're shooting a Western. The bad guy is galloping in front of you on his horse. You're shooting from a camera car. The car hits a bump. Your arm bounces up. The bad guy is no longer in frame. The only thing in frame are a couple of buzzards circling overhead, waiting for the imminent demise of your career. Had you turned on your image stabilizer, you would have been saved. When your arm bounced up, actuators would have told the lens elements to aim down, keeping the cowboy centered in frame.

Optical Stabilization

Optical stabilization has its roots in the 1970s when two optical-mechanical devices were invented: the Dynalens and the ARRI Image Stabilizer. Both attached to the front of existing lenses; they were large and heavy. Built-in gyroscopes adjusted the optical path to compensate for camera movement and shake. The Dynalens was a sandwich of two optical elements with silicon fluid inside. Whenever the camera shook, the elements compensated in the opposite direction. The silicon helped dampen the vibration, but it also degraded the image by diffusing it a little. ARRI's Stabilizer came out a few years later, adapted from British Aerospace technology used in binoculars. It was lighter and didn't soften the image; but wouldn't work on wide-angle lenses. It consisted of mirror pairs that shifted to keep the picture smooth.

DVCAM camcorders have improved on the original concept enormously through miniaturization and electronics. Heavy gyros have been replaced by motion sensors and microprocessors.

Sony's SteadyShot technology actually moves an element inside the zoom lens up-down, left-right in reaction to all your best efforts to make the audience dizzy.

It is helpful to know something about electronic image stabilization, which, although not found on DVCAM camcorders, is the other technology used to make images steady. Developed about 1996, it uses a smaller area on the CCD as the actual picture-taking area. When the camera moves, electronic circuits find a fixed point, like a nose or an eye, and keep it in the same relative position on tape. Electronic stabilization can add noise to the picture, and can also be fooled when you pan or tilt quickly.

Electronic stabilization can also be done in post-production. Be sure to frame a bit wider than the final composition, allowing it to be repositioned frame by frame.

i.LINK - FireWire - IEEE 1394

FireWire and i.LINK are are basically identical, differing in name but not function. It enables DVCAM to possibly be the most open system in broadcast and professional applications, because it lets you plug a DVCAM camcorder into yhour computer to transfer all the video as digital data for editing, emailing, streaming or burning to CD or DVD. And when you're finished editing, the FireWire/i.Link connection lets you plug the camcorderera or VTR into the computer to make a tape of the digitally edited cut.

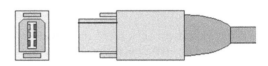

FireWire is the Apple trademark, i.LINK is the Sony term, and IEEE 1394 is the generic industry name for a standard that was agreed upon by a consortium of engineers, making the specs much more complicated than the actual product—which is really just a wire with plugs on each end, and a bunch of technical specs on how the signal should travel down those wires.

i.LINK makes DVCAM possible, because it lets you plug a DVCAM camcorder into your computer to transfer all the video as digital data for editing or emailing. And when you're finished editing, i.LINK lets you plug the camera back into the computer to make a tape from your digitally edited show. However, i.LINK is not just DVCAM—there are IEEE 1394 hard drives, scanners, CD burners, and all kinds of peripherals.

FireWire was invented by Apple Computer in 1986 as a high speed serial bus intended to replace its ADB connectors for keyboards, printers, scanners and other peripherals. But FireWire didn't catch on until 1995, when it appeared under a different, licensed name—i.LINK—on the first DVCAM camcorders from Sony. Apple retained the FireWire trademark.

DVCAM really was the spark that got FireWire/i.LINK going, because it needed faster transfer rates than USB, and SCSI was slower still. In December 1995, FireWire was adopted by the IEEE (Institute of Electrical and Electronics Engineers), and officially called IEEE 1394. FireWire works with both Macs and PCs.

FireWire/i.LINK cables have either 6 or 4 conductors.

The standard FireWire/i.LINK cable has six conductors. Data travels over two individually shielded twisted pairs. Two additional wires carry power (8 to 40 v, 1.5 amp maximum), although they are rarely used. Sony's DSR-250, 300A and 500WS use 6-pin connectors. The DSR-PD100A and DSR-PD150 use 4-pin connec-tors. The 4-conductor cables lack the power wires. Cables with 4 pins on one end and 6 pins on the other are available, as well as 4-4 and 6-6.

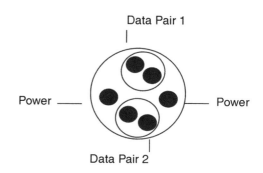

Data Pair 1

Power — Power

Data Pair 2

Cable

The data cable is 28 gauge, and the power pair in the standard cable is 22 gauge. Longer cable runs are possible with thicker cable or by lowering the bit rate. Sony DVCAM camcorders have put out data through FireWire/i.LINK cables at about 100 Megabits per second. So it should be possible to have cables 60 to 90 feet long (20 to 30 meters).

FireWire is not DVCAM. First you buy a DVCAM camcorder. Then you either buy a FireWire/i.LINK/IEEE 1394 equipped computer (Mac or PC), or buy an add-in IEEE 1394 PCI board or PCMCIA card.

Companies that make 1394 cards include Adaptec, Texas Instruments, Radius, ProMax, Canopus, Orange Micro and others.

Multiple Devices

You can, although I've never tried it, connect up to 63 FireWire/i.LINK devices together at one time, provided the cables aren't too long. The 400 Mbps data rate permits simultaneous full-motion, full-frame, 30-frame-per-second video and CD-quality stereo audio. FireWire/i.LINK is Plug and Play, meaning you can plug it in without shutting down the computer.

Up to 63 devices (hard drives, scanners, CD and DVD writers, etc) can be connected simply by connecting them with FireWire/i.LINK cables. ID numbers do not have to be set. Even though they are "daisy-chained," turning off a device does not prevent the next peripheral in line from being used. Devices can be plugged and unplugged at will, and they will be auto-matically recognized. This is called "hot-pluggable."

Data Rates

IEEE 1394/FireWire/i.LINK has a data rate of 100 to 400 Megabits per second, which translates to 40 Megabytes per second, over a 4.5 meter (14') cable.

By comparison, an RS-232 serial port handles 20 kilobits per second, a USB port will move about 12Mbits per second (1.2 Megabytes), and SCSI devices have a data throughput of 5 to 320 Megabytes per second (50 to 3200 Mbits per second).

Data Throughput Speed Chart

Device	Mbps Megabits per second	MB per second MegaBytes per second
FireWire/i.LINK	100-400	10-40
USB	12	1.2
RS-232	.2	.02

SCSI

And then there's SCSI: SCSI, SCSI-2, SCSI-3, Fast SCSI, Fast/Wide SCSI, Ultra SCSI, Wide Ultra SCSI, Ultra2 SCSI, Wide Ultra2 SCSI, and SCSI-3, not to mention Ultra160 and Ultra320.

SCSI Names	8-bit - Narrow	16-bit - Wide
	speeds measured in MegaBytes per second	
SCSI (aka SCSI-1)	5 MB/ps	n/a
Fast, SCSI-2	10 MB/ps	20 MB/ps
Fast-20, SCSI-3, Ultra	20 MB/ps	40 MB/ps
Fast-40, SCSI-4, Ultra2	40 MB/ps	80 MB/ps
Fast-80, Ultra3, Ultra160	80 MB/ps	160 MB/ps
Fast-160, Ultra320	160 MB/ps	320 MB/ps

Sony Contacts

Sony Broadcast & Professional Products Group	Sony Broadcast & Professional Company Sony Electronics Inc. One Sony Drive Park Ridge, NJ 07656 800-686-7669 201-930-1000 www.sony.com/professional www.sonyusadvcam.com
Parts, Manuals, Accessories	Sony Electronics Inc. Business and Professional Group BPG Parts Operations 3300 Zanker Road San Jose, CA 95134-1901 800-538-7550 http://bpcparts.sel.sony.com/
Website for all information on media (DVCAM tape) offered by Sony, where to buy it, information and all kinds of links.	www.mediabysony.com Sony Media Customer Relations 800-942-SONY
Website for the program that rewards users for buying Sony Professional Media. This is the online site to redeem rewards and find useful information about the program.	www.sonyrewardingrecording.com Sony Professional Media Sales Offices: (East) 201 599 3501 (South) 770 662 3803 (West) 714 229 4246

Suppliers

A & J Manufacturing Co. (cases)
11121 Hindry Avenue
Los Angeles, CA 90009
(213) 678-3053800-537-4000
www.ajcases.com

Adobe Systems Inc.
408-536-6000
www.adobe.com

Alfred Chrosziel Film-Technik GMBH
Regerstr. 27
D-8000 Munich 90 Germany
phone: 089-448 03 39 fax: 089-447 08 61

American Society of Cinematographers
1782 North Orange Drive
Hollywood, CA 90028
(213) 876-5080
www.cinematographer.com

Amphibico (underwater housings)
459 Deslauriers
Montreal, Quebec, Canada H4N 1W2
Phone: (514) 333-8666
www.amphibico.com

Anton/Bauer (batteries)
One Controls Drive
Shelton, CT   06484
(203) 929-1100

Apple Computer, Inc.
1 Infinite Loop
Cupertino, CA 95014
408-996-1010
www.apple.com

ARRI USA
617 Route 303
Blauvelt, NY 10913
845-353-1400
www.arri.com

Avid Technology, Inc.
Metropolitan Technology Park
1 Park West
Tewksbury, MA 01876
800-949-AVID
www.avid.com

Birns Sawyer
1026 North Highland Avenue
Hollywood, CA 90038
(213) 466-8211
www.birnsandsawyer.com

Canon USA, Inc.
Broadcast Equipment Div. (Headquarters)
400 Sylvan Avenue
Englewood Cliffs, NJ 07632
(800) 423-LENS / (201) 816-2929
www.usa.canon.com/indtech/
broadcasteq/bctv/

Cartoni USA
10663 Burbank Blvd.
North Hollywood, CA 91601
USA
Phone: +1 (818) 760-8240
www.cartoni.com

Century Precision Optics
11049 Magnolia Blvd
North Hollywood, CA   91601
(818) 766-3715800-228-1254
fax: (818) 505-9865

Cinetech
Karl Horn
719 Arroyo Ave / Unit C
San Fernando, CA 91340
365-0799   fax: (818) 365-8531

Coolzoom (remote zoom controls)
Cool Contraptions
www.coolzoom.com

Focal Press
781-904-2500
www.focalpress.com

Fujinon
973-633-5600
www.fujinonbroadcast.com

Hale Color Consultants (gray scales)
1505 Phoenix Road
Phoenix, MD 21131
(301) 472-4850   (800) 777-1225

Ikelite (underwater housings)
50 West 33rd. Street
Indianapolis, IN 46208
317-923-4523
Fax: 317-924-7988
ikelite@ikelite.com

Jensen Tools Inc.
800-426-1194 or 602-453-3169
www.jensentools.com

Lowel-Light
www.lowel.com

Markertek Video Supply (foam swabs)
145 Ulster Ave
Saugerties, NY 12477
(800) 522-2025   fax: (914) 246-1757

Miller Tripods and Heads
www.miller.com.au/

Matrox Electronic Systems
1055 St. Regis Blvd
Dorval, Quebec Canada, H9P 2T4
800-361-4903
www.matrox.com/videoweb/

Miller-Stephenson MS-943 Safe Zone
Degreaser (replacement for tri-chlor)
203-743-4447   818-896-4714

Nalpak (Magliners, Accessories)
1937-C Friendship Drive
El Cajon, CA 92020
tel: (619) 258-1200 fax: (619) 258-0925

NRG Research Inc. (battery vest)
840 Rogue River Hwy.
Building 144
Grants Pass, OR 97527
503-479-9433

Optex
22-26 Victoria Road
New Barnet, Herts EN4 9PF England
+434 (0) 181 441 2199
www.optexint.com

Pancro Mirrors Inc. (Pancro lens fluid)
818-834-2926
www.pancro.com

Pelican Products
23215 Early Ave.
Torrance, CA 90505
310-326-4700
www.pelican.com

Pinnacle Systems Inc.
280 North Bernardo Ave.
Mountain View, CA 94043
800-474-6622
www.pinnaclesys.com

ProMax
949-727-3977 800-977-6629
www. promax.com

Sachtler Corporation of America
55 N. Main Street
Freeport, NY 11520
(516) 867-4900
and
3316 W. Victory Blvd.
Burbank, CA 91505
(818) 845-4446

Scubacam Ltd
Tel: +(44) 181-987 8681
www.scubacam.co.uk

Seacam Subsea Systems
(underwater housings)
Tel: 714.848.6919 Fax: 714.848.6919
www.seacamsys.com

STE-MAN Inc. (see CARTONI U.S.A.)

The Tiffen Company
90 Oser Ave.
Hauppauge, NY   11788
800-645-2522
www.tiffen.com

Transvideo (LCD TFT Monitors)
10700 Ventura Blvd. #2A
North Hollywood, CA 91604
818-985-4903fax: 818-985-4921
www.transvideointl.com
France: +33 (0) 2 3232 2761
          fax: +33 (0) 2 3260 1479

Vinten Camera Support
www.vinten.co.uk

Wide screen software(SunPath software)
sunPath sun position software for Mac
and PC
widescreen@pobox.com
http://pobox.com/~widescreen

ZGC Inc.(Cooke lenses, Optex in US)
264 Morris Avenue
Mountain Lakes, NJ 07046
973-335-4460
fax: 201-335-4560l
Cooke, Optex, lenses

Tape to Film Facilities (Partial List)

Digital Film Image Transfer Society
http://www.dfits.org/

Black Logic
305 East 46 Street
New York, NY 10017
212-557-2929
www.blacklogic.com

Cineric, Inc. (Solitaire Cine III FLX)
630 Ninth Avenue, Suite 508
New York, NY 10036
212.586.4822 www.cineric.com

Colour Film Services Ltd
10 Wadsworth Road
Perivale, Greenford, Middlesex
UB6 7JX England
Telephone: + 44 (0)20 8998 2731
www.colourfilmservices.co.uk

DuArt Film & Video
245 West 55 Street
New York, NY 10019
212.757.4580 800.52.DuART
www.duart.com

Duboi (Paris)
www.duboi.com

DVFilm
2317 Spring Wagon Ln
Austin, Texas 78728
512-252-2343
http://www.dvfilm.com

EFilm
1146 N. Las Palmas Ave.
Hollywood, CA 90038
323 463-7041
www.efilm.com

Four Media Corporation (4MC)
2820 West Olive Avenue
Burbank, California 91505-4455
818-840-7119 800 423 2652
www.4MC.com

Sony Pictures High Definition Center
(HD to Film)
Culver City, California
35mm Only
310 280 7433 Tel
www.sphdc.com

Swiss Effects
Thurgauerstr. 40
CH-8050 Zurich
Tel. ++41 / 1 / 307 10 10
Fax. ++41 / 1 / 307 10 19
www.swisseffects.ch

Technical Specs

DSR-PD100A Specs

- CCDs: 3x 1/4" 380,000 Pixels
- Lens: 12x Zoom 4.3-51.6mm, f1.6 at 4.3mm, f2.8 at 51.6mm
- Filter size: 52mm
- Image Stabilizer Super SteadyShot (Optical)
- Minimum Illumination: 4 Lux
- 4:3 aspect ratio native chips
- Shutter Speeds: 1/4-1/10,000 sec
- Viewfinder: Color, 180,000 Pixels
- LCD Monitor: 3 1/2" Color, swing out, reversible
- Manual Focus Ring (and Auto)
- Internal Stereo Mic and 1 XLR Audio In w/ phantom power on Hot Shoe
- Power Consumption 4.1 W, W/ Lcd 5.2 W 100/240 V 50/60 Hz
- Dimensions (W/H/D) 3 2/3" x 4" x 7 1/2" (93 x 103 x 198 mm)
- Weight 1 lbs 15 oz (890 g)
- List Price: $2,500

Supplied Accessories

- AC-L10 AC Adapter
- NP-F330 InfoLithium Battery
- RMT-811 Remote Commander
- XLR Adapter, Instruction Manual
- 4 MB Memory Stick; Memory Stick to PC Card Adapter
- Wide Angle Conversion Lens, Lens Hood

Optional Accessories

- NPF-550 InfoLithium Battery
- NPF-750 InfoLithium Battery
- NPF-960 InfoLithium Battery
- BCV-615 Portable Battery Charger
- BCV-500 Dual Battery Charger
- ACV-Q850D AC/DC Power/Battery Charger with Display
- DCCL-50 DC Power Adapter (For Camcorders)
- VCL-R0752 0.7 Wide Angle Lens
- VCL-R2052 2x Telephoto Lens
- VCL-0752H Deluxe 0.7 wide Angle Lens
- VCL-1452H Deluxe 1.4x Telephoto Lens
- ECM-HS1 Zoom Microphone

DSR-PD150 Specs

- CCDs: 3x 1/3" 380,000 pixels
- Lens: 12x Zoom 6-72mm, f1.6 at 6mm, f2.4 at 72mm
- Filter size: 58mm
- Image Stabilizer: Optical Super Steady Shot
- Minimum Illumination: 2 lux (f1.6)
- 4:3 aspect ratio native chips
- ND Filters: 1/4, 1/32
- Shutter Speed: 1/4 to 1/10,000 sec
- Viewfinder: 180,000 dot B&W, 500 lines, 0.4"
- LCD Panel: TFT 200,000 dots, color 2.5" swing-out, reversible display
- Manual Focus Ring (and Auto), Manual Zoom Ring (and Auto)
- Interval Recorder (Time Lapse) 30 seconds/1/5/10 Minute Record Time .5/1/1.5/2 sec
- 2 XLR audio inputs, line/mic select and phantom power
- Accessory Shoe: Cold Shoe
- Power Consumption: 5,4 W with LCD viewing screen
- Power consumption: 4.7 watts with viewfinder only
- Dimensions (W/H/D): 5" x 7 1/8" x 13.5" (125 x 180 x 342mm) w/out Mic
  5 1/8" x 7 1/8" x 16" (128 x 180 x 405mm) with Mic
- Weight body only: 3 lb 8 oz (1.6 kg)
- Weight with NP-F330 battery, tape, mic, lens shade: 3 lb 15 oz (1.8 kg)
- List price $4,000

Supplied Accessories

- AC-L10 AC Adapter
- Directional Mono Microphone ECM-NV1
- Large Eyecup; Standard Eyecup
- Instruction Manual
- 4 MB Memory Stick; USB Memory Stick reader
- NP-F330 Battery
- RMT 811 Remote Control
- ECM-NV1 Monaural Microphone
- Lens Shade; Picture Gear Lite; USB Driver Software; Lens Cap

Optional accessories

- ECM-670PAC - Microphone Package
- MSAC-FD2M Floppy Disk Adapter
- MSAC-PC2 Memory Card Adapter
- NP-F530, 550, 730, 730H, 750, 930, 950, 960 Batteries

DSR-250 Specs

- CCDs: 3x 1/3" 380,000 pixels, interlace for video; progressive for stills
- Lens: 12x 6-72mm, f1.6 at 6mm, f2.4 at 72mm
- Filter size: 58mm
- Shutter Speed: 1/4 to 1/10,000 sec
- Exposure: Auto, Manual
- Viewfinder: DXF-801 1.5" black & white CRT
- Minimum Illumination 2 lux
- LCD Viewing Screen: TFT active matrix, 2.5" (880 x 228)
- ND Filters: 1/4 & 1/32
- Power DC 12V (11 to 17V), 10.5 Watts with viewfinder,
12.1 Watts with viewfinder and LCD
- Dimensions(W/H/D): 9 5/8" x 10" x 20 1/8" (241.7 x 251.2 x 508.8mm)
- Weight 4.4kg 9lb 11oz
- List price $5,900

Supplied Accessories

- RMT 811 Remote Control
- ECM-NV1 Monaural Microphone
- 4 MB Memory Stick; USB Memory Stick Reader
- Lens Shade; Picture Gear Lite; Lens Cap

Optional Accessories

- BP-L40A, BP-L60A, BP-L90A Li-Ion; BP-M50, BP-M100 NiMH Batteries
- BC-M50, BC-L120 Battery Charger
- AC-DN2 AC Adaptor
- QR-DSR Anton Bauer Gold Mount
- HyTRON 50 Anton Bauer NiMH 50 Watt/Hour Battery
- D-2401 Anton Bauer Charger/AC Adaptor
- UL-26 Anton Bauer On Camera Light
- MSA-8A 8MB Memory Stick
- MSA-16A 16MB Memory Stick
- MSA-32A 32MB Memory Stick
- MSA-64A 64MB Memory Stick
- MSAC-PC2 PC Card adaptor for Memory Stick
- MSAC-FD2M Floppy Disk Adaptor for Memory Stick
- VCL-HG1758 Tele Conversion Lens 1.7X
- VCL-HG0758 Wide Conversion Lens 0.7X
- VF-58PK Filter Kit
- VMC-IL4615 1.5m 4-pin to 6-pin i.LINK cable
- VMC-IL6615 1.5m 6-pin to 6-pin i.LINK cable

DSR-300A Specs

- CCD: 3x 1/2" CCDs (4:3)
- Built In Filters: 1: 3200K; 2: 5600K +1/8ND; 3: 5600K; 4: 5600K +1/64ND
- Lens Mount: 1/2" Bayonet Mount
- Horizontal Resolution: 800 Lines, Vertical Resolution 400 Lines
- Minimum illumination: 0.5 Lux at f/1.4, Hyper gain (30dB+DPR)
- Sensitivity: F11 at 2000 Lux
- Gain Selector: -3 dB, 0 dB, + 3 dB, + 6 dB, + 9 dB, + 12 dB, + 18 dB, + 18 dB +DPR, + 24 dB, + 24 dB +DPR, Hyper Gain (30 db+DPR)
- Shutter Speeds: 1/100, 1/250, 1/500, 1/1000, 1/2000 sec.
- S/N Ratio: 62 dB
- Power: DC 12 Volts (11-17v)
- Power Consumption: 22.1 with viewfinder
- Battery Run Time: BP-L40A (80 min), BP-L60A (180 min), BP-L90A (290 min)
- Weight 12 lbs 9 oz (with Viewfinder, Lens, Mic and BP-L40A battery)
- Dynamic Range: More than 80 dB
- Inputs: Genlock Video Input BNC, Time Code Input: BNC
- Mic Input: XLR 3-Pin
- Time Code Output: BNC
- List $9,900.00

Requires 1/2" Bayonet Mount Lens, such as VCL-714BXA (Fujinon), S12x5BRM-38 (Fujinon) or YH18x6.7KRS SY14 (Canon)

Supplied Accessories

- DXF-801 Viewfinder
- Microphone, Instruction Manual
- RM-L61 Remote
- VCT-U14 tripod adapter (mounting plate)

Optional Accessories

- RM-M7G Remote Control Unit, RCP-TX7 Remote Panel
- WRR-855A UHF Synthesized Tuner (wireless mic receiver)
- CA-WR855 Camera Adaptor For WRR-855A
- DSBK-301A Index Picture Board
- DXF-51 5" B/W Viewfinder (Service part A-8274-968-A Required)
- LCR-1 Rain Cover; CAC-12 Microphone Holder
- AC-550 AC Adaptor, AC-DN1 On-Board AC Adaptor (under 38W)
- AC-DN2A AC Adaptor/Charger (for operation under 150W)
- BC-L120, BC-M50 Battery Charger (for Sony Li-ion batteries)
- BP-L40A, BP-L60A, BP-L90A Li-ion; BP-M50, BP-M100 NiMH Batteries
- QRDSR Anton Bauer Gold Mount (required for Anton Bauer Nicad or NiMH batteries)

DSR-500WS Specs

- CCD: 3 x 2/3" 16:9 native (switchable to 4:3)
- Lens Mount: Sony 2/3" Bayonet Mount
- Built In Filters: 3200K; 5600K + 1/8 ND; 5600K; 5600K + 1/64 ND
- Sensitivity: F11 @ 2000 Lux; Minimum Illumination: 0.25 Lux @ 36dB
- Horizontal Resolution: 800 Lines in 16:9 format; 850 lines in 4:3
- Signal To Noise Ratio: 63dB Camera
- Audio Input: Ch 1/Ch 2 (XLR 3-pin Female x 2)
- Time Code In (BNC); Time Code Out (BNC)
- Power Requirements: DC 12V (11 to 17V)
- Power Consumption: 27.1 Watts (With Viewfinder)
- Dimensions: 4 7/8" x 7 5/8" x 11 1/8" (body only)
- Weight: Approx. 13.9 lbs. (With VF, Mic, Battery, and Lens)
- List $16,800

Requires 2/3" Bayonet Mount Lens, such as VCL-918BY, YJ18x9B4 KAS-S12 (Canon) or A19x8.7BRD-S28 (Fujinon)

Supplied Accessories

- DXF-801 Viewfinder
- Microphone, Instruction Manual
- RM-L61 Remote
- VCT-U14 tripod adapter (mounting plate)

Optional Accessories

- RCP-TX7 Remote Control Panel; RM-M7G Remote Control Unit
- WRR-855A UHF Synthesized Tuner (wireless mic receiver)
- CA-WR855 Camera Adaptor For WRR-855A
- DSBK-301A Index Picture Board; DSBK-501 Analog Composite Input Board
- CAC-12 Microphone Holder; LCR-1 Rain Cover
- DXF-51 5" B/W Viewfinder (Service part A-8274-968-A Required)
- AC-550 AC Adaptor
- CMA-8A AC Power Adaptor
- AC-DN1 On-Board AC Adaptor (for operation under 38W)
- AC-DN2A AC Adaptor (for operation under 150W)
- BC-L120, BC-M50 Battery Charger (for Sony Li-ion batteries)
- BP-L40A, BP-L60A, BP-L90A Li-ion Batteries
- BP-M50, BP-M100 NiMH Batteries
- QRDSR Anton Bauer Gold Mount (required for Anton Bauer Nicad or NiMH batteries)

Still Images on Memory Stick: Quantity and Quality

Memory Stick Capacity	Super Fine compression 1/3	Fine compression 1/6	Standard compression 1/10
4MB	20 images	40 images	60 images
8MB	40 images	81 images	122 images
16MB	82 images	164 images	246 images
32MB	164 images	329 images	494 images
64MB	329 images	659 images	988 images

Credits

I would like to extend special thanks to all the people who helped me with this book, generously sharing time and expertise.

At Focal Press, my thanks to Tricia Tyler, publisher, who expertly guided this project from concept to finished product, to Jim DeWolf, VP Technical Division, who make tough logistics possible, and Marie Lee, Exec. Marketing Manager, who supervised the first book and instigated this one. Thanks also to Karen Forster, who handled production, proofreading and details, Cate Barr, Christine Degon and Maura Kelly.

I hope all the people who made this book possible are properly thanked here, although words are inadequate for all the support provided.

My friend Ed Grebow, President, Sony Broadcast and Professional Company, originally thought this book might have merit, paved the way and introduced me to the many incredibly talented and helpful people at the company. Bob Christie was my Sony BPC contact on the last book, and he was one of the first to urge me to do this one. There are many heroes in this project, to whom I am very grateful.

Alec Shapiro, VP Marketing and Communications, spent many hours and much effort rallying support, discussing logistics with Focal Press and me, and ultimately made a project, that had never been done before, a reality.

Wayne Zuchowski, Advertising Manager, and Kristen McNamara, Associate Ad Manager, were given the unenviable additional task of project management, to coordinate all the details, additions, corrections, proofreading and my inevitable 6pm Friday last-minute requests.

Larry Thorpe, VP Aquisition Systems, refined the outline, explained the history, reviewed the text and wrote the foreword with his colleagues.

John Matarazzo, VP Professional Media, was incredibly generous with his time, articulate explanations of tape, and large supply of graphic material. Barbara Ela, Marketing Manager Professional Media, was equally on top of things.

I hope I didn't impose too much on Andy Berger and Craig Yanagi, who answered numerous questions, proofread the text, and showed me the errors of my ways. Geraldine Alvarez was another hero, unflinching whenever yet another request came to ship more equipment for me to evaluate and photograph. Carol Whisker deserves eternal praise for all the Sony BPC photos she provided with the kind folks at Kollins Communication.

I hope I haven't forgotten anyone; the team at Sony BPC were incredible— supplying valuable insight, sharing facts, figures, photos and information: Tony Okada, Mel Medina, Rob Willox, and Bob Ott. Again, my thanks.

I am very grateful to the many friends and colleagues in the industry, not at Sony, who contributed to this book.

Howard Phillips checked the manuscript for errors, and made many helpful contributions.

Michael Phillips at Avid, author of *Digital Filmmaking*—helped me with nonlinear editing, Xpress DV, 24p, and Avid.

Jonathan Morse introduced me to the Olympus E10 digital still camera and taught me how to use it for the pictures in this book.

Thanks to Tom McKay of Varizoom, Bill Meurer, Peter Anway and Ryan Sheridan at Birns and Sawyer.

Saul Molina and Jim McCullaugh at the American Society C were, as always, incredibly helpful and supportive.

Optex and ZGC pictures were supplied by Barbara Lowry of ZGC, Inc. Guy Genin was a valuable resource about lenses.

Bob Carr from Sachtler Corp of America provided photos and tripods for product photography.

Film processing and budgeting help came from Charles Herzfeld of Technicolor.

Help on DVCAM-to-film came from Alfie Schloss of Black Logic in New York, and Patrick Lindenmaier, DP and representative of Swiss Effects. Franz Wieser of ARRI USA provided information and photos for the ARRI Laser.

Dr. James O'Brian instructed me on brain surgery and Sidman.

Special thanks to my ever-patient wife, Noemi, and not-so-impatient daughter, Marlena, who missed out on many weeks of my attention during the production of this book.

Bibliography

In preparing this book, I have used the following sources:

Books

American Cinematographer Manual. ASC Press
Arriflex 16SR Book. Jon Fauer. Focal Press. 1999
Arriflex 35 Book. Jon Fauer. Focal Press. 1999
The Book of Movie Photography. David Cheshire; Dorling Kindersley. 1979
iMovie 2, The Missing Manual. David Pogue. O'Reilly & Assoc
Final Cut Pro for Macintosh. Lisa Brenneis. Peachpit Press
Quicktime Pro for Macintosh & Windows. Stern & Lettieri. Peachpit Press
Digital Filmmaking. Thomas A. Ohanian, Michael E. Phillips. Focal Press
Avid Editing. Sam Kauffmann. Focal Press
The Avid Handbook. Steve Bayes. Focal Press
Every Frame a Rembrandt. Andrew Laszlo, ASC. Focal Press
Writer of Light, Vittorio Storaro, ASC, AIC. Ray Zone. ASC Press
American Cinematographer Video Manual, 3rd Ed. ASC Press

Magazines

American Cinematographer. www.cinematographer.com
Macworld. www.macworld.com
Mac Design. www.macdesignonline.com
Film & Video. www.filmandvideomagazine.com
Res. www.res.com
DV. www.dv.com
Videography. www.videography.com
"Future of Digital Entertainment." *Scientific American*. November 2000.

Internet and Other

"FireWire." B. Schmitt, A. Gerulaitis. www.dvcentral.org/Firewire.html
"FireWire." www.apple.com
"Rallying Around the IEEE 1394." Terence Dyke, Paul Smolen. http://eagle.onr.com/aea/media/tvtech34.html
"MacInTouch FireWire Guide." www.macintouch.com
B&H Photo/Video. New York store and catalog. www.bhphotovideo.com
"Video for Film Release." article by Alan Stewart at www.zerocut.com
"DV Formats." A. Wilt, R. Jennings. www.videouniversity.com/dvformat
"DVCPRO." www.panasonic.com/PBDS/dvcpro_story/index.html
Frank Capria review of editing software at www.dv.com
www.sparcproductdirectory.com/scsiscsi.html
www.24p.com

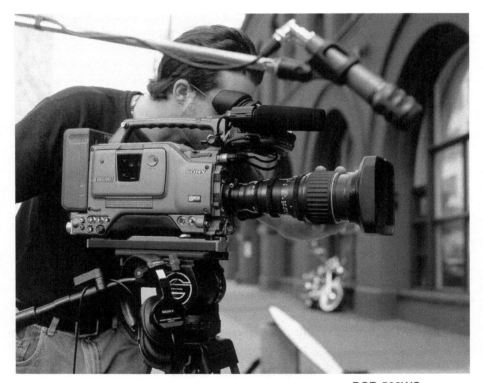

DSR-500WS

Index

About the Author

Jon Fauer has directed and shot hundreds of commercials worldwide. His work includes major campaigns for Sears, Canon, US Coast Guard, Snickers, Mercedes, Buick, Pontiac, Sony, and MCI, featuring the likes of Jennifer Love Hewitt, Lee Iacocca, Naomi Campbell, Jack Nicklaus, Arnold Palmer, Luis Garcia, John McEnroe, and Jesse the Chimpanzee.

He attended schools in Switzerland, graduated from Collegiate School in New York, and received degrees in art and film from Dartmouth College. He studied under Andrew Laszlo, ASC, Maurice Rapf, Joseph Losey and Arthur Mayer.

At Dartmouth he began making medical films as part of his pre-med program, discovered he enjoyed film more than medicine, and, using short-ends to shoot ski films and dramatic short subjects, decided to make a career of it.

His first major film, *Wildwater*, commissioned by U.S. Kayak Team coach Jay Evans, featured the World Whitewater Championships in Merano, Italy. That film, and the numerous awards it won, led to documentaries around the world in the jungles of Guatemala, the mountains of New Zealand, and the Altiplano of Bolivia; from the North Pole for *American Sportsman* to the Chesapeake for *National Geographic*. His work led to membership in The Explorers Club of New York.

He got his first break in the business from Mel London, filmmaker and author of countless books on film and fine cooking.

Documentary camerawork led to feature films and TV commercials. Among other credits, Fauer was Director of Photography on *Tales from the Darkside* and the title sequence for *Bonfire of the Vanities;* camera operator on *Splash* and *St. Elmo's Fire*; 2nd Unit Director of Photography on *All the Right Moves* and *Remo Williams*.

He is a member of the Explorers Club, Directors Guild of America, International Cinematographers Guild and the American Society of Cinematographers.

Fauer lives in New York City and Southampton, NY, with his wife and daughter.

Focus Charts

Photocopy these focus charts and use them to check focus and back focus of your lenses. See page "Adjust Back Focus" on page 119

For Product Safety Concerns and Information please contact our EU
representative GPSR@taylorandfrancis.com
Taylor & Francis Verlag GmbH, Kaufingerstraße 24, 80331 München, Germany

www.ingramcontent.com/pod-product-compliance
Ingram Content Group UK Ltd.
Pitfield, Milton Keynes, MK11 3LW, UK
UKHW021007180425
457613UK00019B/841